His Name

Seeking and Finding the Treasures of the Hebraic Roots of our Faith

Leo Vanderploeg

Much appreciation to Rick Dees, Nigel Butler and Gary Stevenson who have proof read the document and gave me advice before the publication of this writing. All errors of judgement are mine.

Dedicated to my friends Gary and Fiona Stevenson
who were partially responsible in inspiring me to write
this little book.

Published and printed by lulu.com

Front and back cover design: Jason Fell
Front cover image: Dead sea scroll, Public Domain
Back cover image: Western Wall, Jerusalem CC Gilabrand at en.wikipedia

Massive thanks go to Jason Fell for the final computer formatting and designing of this book.

כִּי הַנֹּגֵעַ בָּכֶם נֹגֵעַ בְּבָבַת עֵינוֹ

Anyone who injures you [**צִיּוֹן** Tzion] injures the very pupil of my eye.

זְכַרְיָה Zechariah 2:12

אִם־אֶשְׁכָּחֵךְ יְרוּשָׁלָ͏ִם תִּשְׁכַּח יְמִינִי

If I forget you, Yerushalayim, may my right hand wither away!

תְהִלִּים Psalms 137:5

שַׁאֲלוּ שְׁלוֹם יְרוּשָׁלָ͏ִם יִשְׁלָיוּ אֹהֲבָיִךְ

Pray for the peace of Yerushalayim and may those who love you prosper.

תְהִלִּים Psalms 122:6

Contents

Part One

Part Two

Preface

Initially I was planning to write a very short paper just on why 'Jesus' is not a suitable name for The One who created the world and who we are to worship, because that is not his real name. I attempted to trace the origins of the name 'Jesus' and the reason why many people still use the name today. This is *part one*. As I researched this topic other concerns arose which I have labelled in this writing as *part two*. The list in part two is not an exhaustive list. As this goes to print, other concerns come to mind, but perhaps I have addressed some of the more important ones. The goal of part two in this essay is to make the reader aware that the Greek mentality in an approach to studying scripture differs greatly to Hebraic hermeneutics and exegesis. I am also hoping to assist the reader to being aware of these better Hebraic tools for studying the Bible. In addition it has become clear to me that the church has not made the Jew very jealous (Romans 11:11) for the gospel. Perhaps we can make steps to amend this situation and I have suggested a few things we could do. I hope this volume will help in this regard. I am hoping to arouse the reader to pick up some of my ideas and do some research of his/her own. If I make any 'alarming' comments be assured my intention is to not offend anyone but to spur us on to being better Messianic followers of Yeshua.

This writing may be a bit difficult to follow for those unfamiliar with Hebrew script and Jewish words. I trust that Jewish friends who are acquainted with the Hebrew language and culture will find this information greatly acceptable and most welcome. My purpose in this little book is to assist those, particularly Gentile friends who are very unfamiliar with Hebrew words or phrases, to become familiar with some of them, and recognise the profound biblical history and importance of the Hebrew language and the Jewish roots that we have been grafted into (Romans 11). I believe that we need to get acquainted with our Jewish brothers and sisters and their culture. By the time you have finished reading this paper I am hoping you will understand the great significance of Judaism. I am strongly influenced by biblical English translations written by Rabbis and Jews as they reveal the great richness and depth of words and phraseology that we Gentiles should learn. For instance, Hebrew does not have a 'J' sound so we say Yisra'el (Israel) and Yerushalayim (Jerusalem). Church, Christians and Christianity will always refer to non-Jews – when you are done reading this writing I'm sure you will understand why. For those not familiar with the Hebrew script, it is read right to left unlike Greek and English script. All scripture quotations in English are from David Stern's *Complete Jewish Study Bible* but I often replace his use of Adonai with the Hebrew name Yehovah, as it appears in the Hebrew text. Stern rightly uses the name 'Yeshua' and 'Torah' but I often add to these English words the Hebrew script (as I am hoping that the reader will get acquainted to the Hebrew Script with certain often used words). I also replace his use of Isra'el for the more accurate word Yisra'el. The reason for these changes will become apparent later as I get further into this document. When I am quoting someone and I add a comment within the quote or correct their use of 'Jesus' or 'Old or New Testament' I always enclose the remark or addition with these brackets [ ]. Where the numbering of Hebrew Bible verses differs from English translations I prefer and use the Hebrew text.

Monographs that have dealt seriously with the origin of the name 'Jesus' are very few[1]. But none that I am aware of, have ever contemplated a replacement theology/anti-Semitic connection as to why the correct Hebrew name יֵשׁוּעַ Yeshua is ignored. The time is long overdue for a careful critique on this aspect and I see this paper as at least a start in addressing this deficiency and probing a subject matter not often considered. Hopefully others will take up the trail

1 I have one book: Roger Sapp, 2012, USA, Jehovah, Yahweh, Jesus or Yeshua? Does it Really Matter? But I certainly cannot recommend his book.

and see where it leads – so may this work be the first of a number of writings on the origins of the name of יֵשׁוּעַ Yeshua.

Part One

Years ago when I began studying Hebrew, I soon learned that Jesus' name was יֵשׁוּעַ Yeshua (pronouncing the name with emphasis on the shu part). יֵשׁוּעַ Yeshua is pleasant sounding, is easy to say and I have pondered for a long time why do we not use יֵשׁוּעַ Yeshua's real name. As I accumulated more and more Jewish articles, commentaries and books and attended Jewish conferences which use יֵשׁוּעַ Yeshua's name, I have become much more concerned.

I remember the days when I worked in India, Africa and particularly my longer stay in China. I learned that names matter. Much more than our American/British culture – names have important meanings and are carefully chosen. The characters (such as in Chinese script, and also the sound the character makes) are not picked at random but carefully chosen. When one is to meet someone of higher rank or status than you, such as a teacher or dignitary – it is imperative that you would practice the persons real name before you meet them. The better you pronounced their name (or at least gave an impression of a concerted effort on your part) which showed them your respect – the more impressed they were with you, and the more respect you received as they were pleased with you.

So this is the background for the question – why don't we use יֵשׁוּעַ Yeshua's real name. Obviously יֵשׁוּעַ Yeshua is not just anyone. יֵשׁוּעַ Yeshua was the Jew we read about – born 2000 years ago. He was the one who the First Covenant (known inaccurately as the Old Testament but from now on will be referred to as First Covenant or Torah) pointed to. יֵשׁוּעַ Yeshua was born to renew God's covenant with His Jewish people. יֵשׁוּעַ Yeshua actually is our creator, maker of heaven and earth. He is our Lord God יהוה Yehovah![2] He is the Word and our Light and Life (John 1:1-5). Matthew 1:21 says, "She will have a son, and you will name him יֵשׁוּעַ Yeshua because He will יוֹשִׁיעַ Yoshiya (save) His people from their sins." We now know these Hebrew words were spoken and that the Greek here is a translation of an original Hebrew manuscript, so no one can legitimately question the words or names used here.[3]

We pronounce Abraham אַבְרָהָם (Avraham), Lot לוֹט (Lot with the 'o' sound as in low), Ruth רוּת (Rut), David דָּוִד (David with the 'a' sound as in father) etc. very similar to the rules of Hebrew phonetics with no problem; the transliterations are not bad – so what happened with Yeshua? So again the big question – why on earth would we still be using 'Jesus' instead of what we know to be his real and proper name – יֵשׁוּעַ Yeshua.

Hebrew background for יֵשׁוּעַ Yeshua

Hebrew עִבְרִי (ev'ri) is one of the world's oldest languages deriving from עֵבֶר (Ever), the son of Shem[4] (Gen 10:21). That puts the date roughly 2446 BC.[5] In perspective, as creation happened about 4000 BC, no language can be older than creation. Also in the land of Canaan, before Shem, a

2 I will write about the name Yehovah later in this paper.

3 Nehemia Gordon and Keith Johnson, A Prayer To Our Father, 2010, p. 117; see also many of Nehemia Gordon's YouTube presentations.

4 Al Garza, The Hebrew New Testament, The Jewish Institute, 2012, p. 9; George M. Lamsa, New Testament Origin, The Aramaic Bible Society, 2004, p. 56.

5 Larry and Marion Pierce, The Annals of the World, USA, 2005, p. 19.

'proto-Canaanite' language was spoken and Abraham's clan in Egypt (Gen 15:13) spoke a Canaanite variant. From this the Phoenician script developed – this being similar to the proto-Hebrew script (also called early Aramaic Script).[6] Douglas Petrovich, an ancient-inscription specialist concurs saying Hebrew contains the oldest alphabet in the world.[7] Nehemia Gordon[8] makes a good case showing that the 'one language' mentioned in Genesis 11:1 had to be Hebrew.[9] For instance, the reason for the names of people – they relate only in Hebrew. For example, **אָדָם** (Adam) was formed from the ground **אֲדָמָה** (adama) – Genesis 2:7; Adam to the women said, "she shall be called women **אִשָּׁה** (isha) because she was taken out of man **אִישׁ** (ish)" – Genesis 2:23. The man called his wife חַוָּה (chava) because she was the mother of all living **חָי** (chai) humans – Genesis 3:20. Adam's wife gave birth to **קַיִן** (Qayin[10]) Cain and said I have acquired **קָנִיתִי** (qanete – from **קנה** qna[11]) a man – Genesis 4:1. **הָבֶל** (Havel) Abel (Genesis 4:2) means vanity/emptiness[12] (**קַיִן** Qayin killed הָבֶל Havel). **פֶּלֶג** Peleg

---

6 Al Garza, p. 10-12; Nehemia Gordon and Keith Johnson, pp. 37-42.

7 Douglas Petrovich, The Jerusalem Post, January, 2017, p. 17.

8 Nehemia Gordon holds a Masters Degree in Biblical Studies and a Bachelors Degree in Archaeology from the Hebrew University of Jerusalem. Fluent in Hebrew, Gordon has worked extensively with ancient manuscripts and on the publication and translation of the Dead Sea Scrolls. Currently he lectures on Tanach and Hebrew Renewed Covenant topics around the world, leads tours to Israel and is continuing research on the Hebrew sources of the Renewed Covenant.

9 Nehemia Gordon, YouTube, Minding my own business, July 7, 2014; Nehemia Gordon and Keith Johnson, 2010, see the whole book but particularly p. 42.

10 Which can also mean 'to provoke to jealousy' or envious, Strong's Hebrew/Chaldee Dictionary, entry 7069, 7065; or lament, entry 6969; or sense of fixity, entry 7013.

11 Strong's Hebrew/Chaldee Dictionary, entry 7069.

12 Strong's Hebrew/Chaldee Dictionary, entry 1892.

(Genesis 10:25) means division because during his lifetime the earth was divided נִפְלְגָה (nif'lega).

Though the language has gone through three basic periods – biblical, mishnaic and medieval, the Hebrew language is still used today. The rebirth of Hebrew as a spoken language occurred after 1881 and is now the spoken language of modern Israel.[13] Hebrew has always been regarded as לָשׁוֹן הַקָּדוֹשׁ (Lashon ha-kodesh), the sacred language of the people, and תּוֹרָה Torah[14] was very sacred. Ezra (sometime after 538 BC[15]) established תּוֹרָה Torah readings in Hebrew every Sabbath for all synagogues and required Hebrew to be used for all Jewish rituals.[16] We see Ezra's influence right up to today.

יֵשׁוּעַ Yeshua, his family being devoutly Jewish (Luke 2:39-42) would have been given a good Jewish education.[17] The main subjects יֵשׁוּעַ Yeshua would have studied were תּוֹרָה Torah and the Oral תּוֹרָה Torah[18]. It was expected that by age 13 the students would know their subjects well, committing to memory immense portions of תּוֹרָה Torah overseen by the Pharisees. We see the evidence of this when

---

13 Al Garza, p. 15.

14 תּוֹרָה Torah can refer to the first five books of Moses or it can refer to all of the Hebrew Scriptures (known as the Old Testament) or it can also include the Oral Law – but when I refer to Torah it will always mean all of the Hebrew Scriptures (also referred to as The First Covenant or The Original Covenant).

15 Sometime after perhaps 538 B.C. (New Bible Dictionary, 3rd ed., I. H. Marshall, A. R. Millard, J. I. Packer & D. J. Wiseman,2010, England, p. 356; The Jewish Study Bible, 2nd ed., 2014, Oxford, p. 1661)

16 Al Garza, p. 17.

17 Al Garza, p. 18. See also Revd Frank Andrews, Is There Death in the Pot, 2012, UK, pp. 16-30.

18 The Oral Torah will be explained later in part two.

יֵשׁוּעַ Yeshua is 12 years old as He is astounding his teachers [19] in יְרוּשָׁלַיִם Yerushalayim [20] (Luke 2:46-47). Another source says this: age 5 – study written תּוֹרָה Torah; age 10 – study Mishnah (Oral תּוֹרָה Torah/commentary[21]); age 13 – Bar Mitzvah; age 15 – study Talmud.[22] Does this seem far fetched? Today, the Hasidim of New York, as advocated by 12th century Maimonides, insist boys begin their study of Hebrew at age three and in their fourth year, start learning תּוֹרָה Torah. Six days a week, boys rise at 3 or 3:30 in the morning to go to mikvah (the ritual bath), then they are in school from 5:30 or 6 a.m. until sundown, and after that return to the synagogue etc.[23] Furthermore, it can be noted "that Galilee, where Yeshua was educated and raised, was actually more devoted, as a whole, to the study and practice of the Torah than many parts of Judah."[24]

There is overwhelming textual evidence that יֵשׁוּעַ Yeshua spoke Hebrew. Indeed it is becoming apparent that the whole Renewed Covenant (known also as the New Testament) we read in Greek, is actually a translation from the original Hebrew manuscripts.[25] This would be expected, as in the time of יֵשׁוּעַ Yeshua and שָׁאוּל (Sha'ul) Paul the

19 Kelvin Crombie, Israel, Jesus and Covenant, 2017, Australia, pp. 209-210; Marvin R. Wilson, Our Father Abraham, 1989, USA, pp. 298-299.

20 Or יְרוּשָׁלַם Yerushalam

21 There will be lots on this later.

22 David Bivin, New Light on the Words of Jesus, 2007, USA, p. 4. See also Rabbi Adin Even-Israel Steinsaltz, Reference Guide to the Talmud, pp. 25-27.

23 Wilson, Our Father Abraham, p. 301.

24 David Friedman, They Loved The Torah, 2001, USA, p. 11.

25 Nehemia Gordon and Keith Johnson, 2010; see also many of Nehemia Gordon's YouTube presentations; Al Garza, pp. 19-40, 49-54; Brad Young, Meet the Rabbis, 2010, pp. 10, 83; Lois Tverberg, Walking in the Dust of Rabbi Jesus, 2012, USA, p. 205 #4.

Greek language and culture were quite repulsive to the Jews – they thought it would be better to eat pigs than to learn Greek. Hebrew was indeed the sacred tongue.[26] This attests to the fact that at present there are 28 Hebrew manuscripts of Matthew in existence;[27] also the Soviet Union (St. Petersburg) has the largest selection of Hebrew manuscripts in the world, thousands of which now have been microfilmed. Nehemia Gordon was even studying the Renewed Covenant or בְּרִית חֲדָשָׁה B'rit Chadashah (known inaccurately as the New Testament but from now on will be referred to as R.C.) book of Revelation in Hebrew![28]

The French scholar and archaeologist Ernest Renan believed that יֵשׁוּעַ Yeshua could not have known Greek as this language was very little spread in Judea beyond the classes who participated in the government and the towns inhabited by pagans, like Caesarea.[29] And Lamsa likewise said that Greek was seldom spoken in Israel (except by a few government officials). The daily language spoken was Aramaic and the literary language was Hebrew (he believed all שָׁאוּל Paul's references to Greeks are actually referring to Arameans/Syrians),[30] but there seems to be more scholars, like Brad Young[31], who believe יֵשׁוּעַ Yeshua

---

26 George M. Lamsa, New Testament Origin, p. 39, additional reading pp. 30-35.

27 Nehemia Gordon and Keith Johnson, p. 41.

28 Nehemia Gordon, Hebrew Matthew and the Lord's Prayer, YouTube, Dec. 2017; Nehemia Gordon and Keith Johnson, pp. 117-119.

29 Lamsa, pp. 22-23.

30 Ibid., pp. 32-35.

31 Brad Young is one of those rare cases where a Gentile can break the language barrier moving freely in Hebrew and Aramaic sources of early Judaism proficiently. Written on cover of his book, 'The Parables' and a

could probably carry on a conversation in Greek, speak Arabic (Arabic is similar to Hebrew) but when teaching preferred Hebrew.[32] Rabbi Adin Even-Israel Steinsaltz's view is that in the mishnaic period and even in the talmudic period (30 BC-500 AD), the spoken and written language of the common people was probably Hebrew.[33]

David Stern who translated the Renewed Covenant into English and wrote the important book, 'Messianic Jewish Manifesto,' reminds us Gentiles that the R.C.

> is in fact a Jewish Book – by Jews, mostly about Jews, and for Jews as well as Gentiles. It is all very well to adapt a Jewish book for easier appreciation by non-Jews, but not at the cost of suppressing its inherent Jewishness. The *Jewish* **בְּרִית חֲדָשָׁה** B'rit Chadashah or R.C. expressed this Jewishness first of all in its very name...[34]
>
> For the central figure...**יֵשׁוּעַ** Yeshua the Messiah...was a Jew, born into a Jewish family in Beit-Lechem (Bethlehem), grew up among the Jews in **נְצֶרֶת** Nazaret (Nazareth), ministered to the Jews in **גָּלִיל** Galil (Galilee), and died and rose from the grave in the Jewish capital, **יְרוּשָׁלַיִם**

---

comment by Nehemia Gordon on YouTube; Eli Lizorkin-Eyzenberg, The Jewish Gospel of John, 2015, Israel, p. 138.

32 Brad H. Young, Meet The Rabbis, 2007, USA, p. 10.

33 Rabbi Adin Even-Israel Steinsaltz, Reference Guide to the Talmud, Second, revised edition, 2014, pp. 22-23.

34 As the renewed covenant – most of the covenants of the Torah are written solely to the Jewish people, so that Jewishness is expressed right in the name. The First covenant and the second renewed covenant are as one book, one Torah.

> Yerushalayim (Jerusalem) – all in אֶרֶץ יִשְׂרָאֵל Erets Yisra'el (the land of Israel), the land God gave to the Jewish people. Moreover, Yeshua is still a Jew, since he is still alive; and nowhere does Scripture say or suggest that he has stopped being Jewish. His twelve closest followers were Jews. For years all his תַּלְמִידִים talmidim (disciples) were Jews, eventually numbering 'tens of thousands' in Yerushalayim alone (Acts 21:20). The [R.C.] was written entirely by Jews (Luke being, in all likelihood, a proselyte to Judaism); and its message is directed 'to the Jew especially, but equally 'to the Gentile' (Rom. 1:16). It was the [יְהוּדִים Yehudim[35]] Jews who brought the gospel to non-Jews, not the other way around…[36]

His תַּלְמִידִים talmidim (disciples) called Him רַבִּי Rabbi[37] (John 4:31, 20:16) as did others (John 3:2, 6:25). יֵשׁוּעַ Yeshua even said that 'salvation is from the Jews' שֶׁהֲרֵי הַיְשׁוּעָה מֵאֵת הַיְּהוּדִים. The R.C. is made to the 'House of Israel,' not to the Gentiles! (Jeremiah 31:30). Much more can be written about this but I'm sure my point is clear: the whole תּוֹרָה Torah, including the בְּרִית חֲדָשָׁה R.C. ('whole תּוֹרָה Torah' in this writing will mean both covenants – the Tanach and the R.C.[38]) constitute our Christian roots and both are Jewish and Hebraic. יֵשׁוּעַ Yeshua was a יְהוּדִי

35 Pronounced Yehudeem

36 Stern, The Complete Jewish Study Bible, 2016, Hendrickson Publishers, p. xliv-xlv.

37 See also David Bivin, New Light on the Words of Jesus, pp. 9-10; Eli Lizorkin-Eyzenberg, The Jewish Gospel of John, p. 17.

38 Stern advocates that as believers in Yeshua, we can use the word Torah as referring to our whole canon of scripture – the First Covenant and the R.C. (David H. Stern, Messianic Jewish Manifesto, 1991, p. 146).

Yehudi[39] (Jew), is a יְהוּדִי Yehudi and is coming again as a יְהוּדִי Yehudi;[40] He's not returning to London or New York, but to אֶרֶץ יִשְׂרָאֵל Erets Yisra'el[41] (the land of Israel) (Acts 1:11; Revelation 14:1, 21:1-3, 10). יֵשׁוּעַ Yeshua was born king of the יְהוּדִים Yehudim Jews (Matthew 2:2) and died king of the יְהוּדִים Yehudim Jews (Mark 15:2, 26) and will return as King of the יְהוּדִים Yehudim (Micah 5:2; Isaiah 60:3; Psalm 89:21, 28, 30; Revelation 19:6-9).

So now back to the question – why on earth are we calling יֵשׁוּעַ Yeshua 'Jesus'? Even הַשָּׂטָן the satan[42] got to keep his name. So I think we have a serious problem. Here below is the common reason given for the origin of Jesus:

Origin of the name 'Jesus'

Around 330 BC the Greeks were taking over the Middle East. Greek eventually became the dominant international language, though of course the Jews continued speaking and studying Hebrew. When the R.C. was being written and the gospel of יֵשׁוּעַ Yeshua was reaching the Gentiles, there was a need to translate the Hebrew manuscripts to Greek. To *translate* proper names – one can bring across the meaning of a name, so יֵשׁוּעַ Yeshua could have been called 'God saves'. Another method is to *transliterate* – to bring across the sound of the name. If down through history

39 Pronounced Yehudee.

40 See also, Ilse Posselt, The Jerusalem Post, October 2016, 29 col 3. (Rev 5:5) Yeshua as being a lion from the tribe of Judah - meaning His Jewishness is anything but temporary but eternal.

41 See also Rabbi Barney Kasdan, Messianic Commentary on Matthew, 2011, USA, pp. 301-305.

42 In Hebrew 'satan' always appears with the definite article: the satan. M. S. Heiser, The Unseen Realm, 2015, USA, p. 57.

scholars had transliterated יֵשׁוּעַ Yeshua differently He would have received the name Joshua because Joshua in the תּוֹרָה Torah and יֵשׁוּעַ Yeshua in the R.C. are the same.

Usually transliterating is an easy process, but in the case of יֵשׁוּעַ Yeshua there were four problems for the ancient Greeks. They did not have the 'Y' (as in yet) sound for the י yod in יֵשׁוּעַ, nor the 'sh' (as in shop) sound for the שׁ shin. So the Greek Iησους (ee-ay-soos/Iêsous)[43] was formed – the Iη iota & eta were put together to produce the a (as in ate) sound and the δ sigma replaced the Hebrew שׁ. But masculine Greek names cannot end in a vowel in the nominative case so another ς sigma was added. That is why, for example, Juda became Judas, Cephah became Cephas, Apollo – Apollas, Barnabie – Barnabas, Matthew – Matthias. Finally, the last two vowel sounds in Hebrew וּעַ vav & ayin do not flow in Greek so the ע ayin was dropped. So now the new invented name Iησους Iêsous robbed יֵשׁוּעַ Yeshua of all of its meaning and most of its sound.[44]

Around 400 AD Latin became the dominant language, so the Greek R.C. was translated into Latin. This translation was called The Latin Bible or Vulgate. It transliterated Iησους to IESUS (identical in pronunciation) easily enough, as Latin had all the necessary sounds. The Latin spelling and pronunciation continued for almost 1000 years. The English language, meanwhile, was evolving. For example, the letter 'J', never existing in Hebrew, Aramaic, Greek, or Latin, appeared in the 12th century. But it still took over 500 years for the I and Y to be finally replaced by a 'J'. The

43 Oo as in soon.
44 Scott Nelson, How the Name Yeshua Became Jesus, www.judaismvschristianity.com/how_the_name.htm

1384 translation from the Vulgate by John Wycliffe still used Iesus.[45] All proper names in the whole תּוֹרָה Torah were transliterated into English according to their Hebrew pronunciation but when English pronunciation shifted or changed to what we know today, these transliterations were unfortunately not changed to suit the new pronunciations. So the Hebrew names Yerushalayim, Yeriho and Yarden became known to us as Jerusalem, Jericho, Jordan.[46] Yona, Iames and Yohan became Jonah, James and John. Then, in the 1450's the printing press was invented. When William Tyndale translated the R.C. in 1526 from the Vulgate along with Greek manuscripts he was the first to use the letter 'J' to spell Jesus.[47] But it would have been pronounced then as Yesus.

By the 17th century, the letter 'J' being officially part of the King's English, the King James Bible (KJB) employed the name Jesus.[48] Nehemia Gordon says that the original KJB 1611 used the 'J' and 'I' interchangeably (and also made use of the name Yehovah). It was not until 1634 that a distinction between these two letters was consistent.[49] When the name Jesus first appeared in Germany, the letter 'J' was used as a 'Y' but the French pronounced the 'J' hard. This hard 'J' pronunciation influenced the English speakers pronouncing Jesus like we do today.[50] The 'oo' sound (as in soon) of Iesus also disappeared. As we see – the name

---

45 Ibid., Scott Nelson

46 David Bivin, How Yeshua became Jesus, adapted by Bridges for Peace, https://jesusisajew.org/YESHUA.php

47 Scott Nelson.

48 Ibid.

49 Nehemia Gordon and Keith Johnson, p. 102.

50 David Wilkerson, Is it Jesus, Yeshua, Yeshu...and does it matter?, YouTube

Jesus is a very recent development in the English language; less than 350-400 years.[51] But as Meyer says, it took many years more for the name to be known as Jesus [as the name had to spread slowly throughout Europe and then to the other continents of the world – although many places never adopted the name]. I suspect that for many areas the name 'Jesus' is perhaps less than 300 years old!

Unfortunately the ee sound of 'JE'-sus remained. Later English speakers wrongly interpreted that יֵשׁוּעַ Yeshua began with the ee sound instead of the 'Yeh'. Concerning the last 'sh' sound in יֵשׁוּעַ Yeshua, translators of English versions of the R.C. transliterated the Greek transcription of a Hebrew name, instead of turning to the original Hebrew (which they should have done). David Bivin says that "this was doubly unfortunate, first because the 'sh' sound exists in English, and second because in English the 's' sound can shift to the 'Z' sound, which is what happened in the case of the pronunciation of 'Jesus'".[52]

Almost all Jewish names have a literal meaning, like יֵשׁוּעַ Yeshua meaning יְהֹוָה Yehovah saves. In comparison the name Ιησους (Iêsous) never existed in Greek and the name Jesus never existed before 400 years ago, i.e. they both have **no** meaning. Stern comments that in Matthew 1:21, an angel of יְהֹוָה Yehovah

> tells יוֹסֵף Yosef that מִרְיָם Miriam (Mary), his betrothed, will give birth to a son, 'and you are to name Him יֵשׁוּעַ Yeshua, because He will יוֹשִׁיעַ

---

51 Scott Nelson.

52 David Bivin, Adapted from an article by David Bivin with kind permission of Bridges for Peace, https://jesusisajew.org/YESHUA.php

> Yoshiya (save) His people from their sins.' In English the reason explains nothing – why not name Him 'George, because he will save his people from their sins'? Likewise, in Greek – the name Ιησους Iêsous has nothing to do with sotêr, the Greek word for 'save'. Only in Hebrew or Aramaic can the explanation explain. The Hebrew name יֵשׁוּעַ Yeshua, which is the masculine form of the word yeshu'ah (ישׁועה – 'salvation'), is based on the same root (yud-shin-'ayin – י-שׁ-ע) as יושׁיע yoshia, which means 'he will save.'[53]

Bivin comments, "Through multiple translations and changes in pronunciation, a tradition of saying 'Jesus' has obscured His name, 'Yeshua'. It has shifted His perceived message and identity from Hebrew to Greek."[54]

With all the above reasons just listed for the cause of the name change, another huge problem persists. Why did Joshua, who shared the same Hebrew and Greek names as 'Jesus' did, now have a hugely diverse path? Joshua went through the same mess of transliterations as יֵשׁוּעַ Yeshua did. Fortunately his name changed little but somehow יֵשׁוּעַ Yeshua lost out. I suggest that this is infuriating. Lex Meyer wrote that some people

> claim that His name was changed to Jesus to hide the fact that He was a Jew, since Jesus is based on a Greek name rather than a Hebrew name. While it is possible that there might be some truth to this claim, it is far fetched to think that it was some

53 Stern, The Complete Jewish Study Bible, p. xlv.
54 How Yeshua became Jesus, https://jesusisajew.org/YESHUA.php

grand conspiracy to hide the Jewishness of Jesus, since the Bible clearly says that He was a Jew.[55]

Well I am about to show you that indeed there was a conspiracy! Or perhaps even greater than a conspiracy, there was a complete affront, contempt, hatred and hostility to a Hebrew יֵשׁוּעַ Yeshua!

If you go to YouTube and search for 'How Yeshua became Jesus', you will find many entries. Some good – some not-so-good. But they all miss one huge ingredient that changes the outcome of the whole argument. That is no one has considered the effects of replacement theology and the effects of anti-Semitism on the origin of the name 'Jesus'. And this is where we now turn.

Replacement Theology

There are many books written on this subject but I am going to refer mainly to two books which I recommend if you haven't seen them before. Israel and the Church (The Origin and Effects of Replacement Theology)[56] and The Jews, Modern Israel and the New Supersessionism[57]. Here I present a skeletal review.

The gospel, originating in Yerushalayim, as mentioned previously was founded thoroughly in Judaism. The culture, language, and thinking were all Jewish. But יִשְׂרָאֵל Yisra'el

---

55 Lex Meyer, How Yeshua became Jesus, http://unlearnthelies.com/how-yeshua-became-jesus.html

56 Ronald E. Diprose, Israel and the Church, 2004, Rome, Italy.

57 Calvin L. Smith, editor, The Jews, Modern Israel and the New Supersessionism, 2013, UK.; another good book is: Revd Frank Andrews, Is There Death in the Pot.

was controlled by the hated Romans and in 66 AD Jewish Zealots rebelled against them. The result was that Titus (in 70 AD) destroyed most of Yerushalayim, the second temple and was responsible for the deaths of around one million Jews. In 135 AD the Jews again revolted; this time a further half a million Jews were slaughtered, Yerushalayim was totally destroyed and the Jews were exiled. During this period, both Christianity and Judaism experienced hostility because both were monotheistic and opposed the use of images (the Greeks and Romans had many gods and made use of many images). For any remaining or returning Jews the struggle for survival produced a spirit of rivalry between the two groups.[58] Christians soon developed their own identity, and with the lack of a Jewish presence, began to lead the assemblies. With the coming of Christ they started to think that Yerushalayim and the Jews had served their purpose, and began distancing themselves from their Jewish roots; from Judaism.

Christianity was embracing the new incoming Greco-Roman culture; a culture totally foreign and antagonistic to Judaism. Already by 115 AD Ignatius of Antioch told his readers to oppose all things Jewish. Christians also began to appropriate to themselves what was originally addressed to Yisra'el; embracing an allegorical interpretation of the Bible. Allegory is a way of representing a situation and giving it meaning which is not the literal meaning. Therefore for an evolutionist (one who believes that the earth is billions of years old) he must make the statements of the Bible (which demand a young earth in terms of

58 Calvin Smith, editor, Horner, chpt 2 in The Jews, Modern Israel and the New Supersessionism, pp. 37-38; Hugh Kitson, Jerusalem the Covenant City, 2000, UK, pp. 70, 73; Diprose, Israel and the Church, pp. 69-70.

thousands of years) to mean something other than their literal meaning, to accommodate his millions of years. For the Jewish question, all references in the Bible to a literal Yerushalayim, covenants, or the Jewish people, would have to be interpreted differently – avoiding the literal interpretation. In short, everything that actually applied to Yisra'el, now applied to the church. This false interpretation of the תּוֹרָה Torah, of course, increased the rivalry between the two communities. The allegorical interpretation of the Bible has its roots in the Greek anti-Christian philosophy of Socrates, and Plato who was known for his love of allegory, along with Aristotle. These men's writings were extremely influential for the future of the church.[59] This is seen in Justin Martyr's work when he used the word 'Spiritual Israel' (which does not exist in the Bible). Christians, he says, are the true Israelite race, as he believed the Church replaced Isra'el; concepts in the תּוֹרָה Torah he applied indiscriminately to the church. Justin also showed contempt for circumcision and the Jews as a people. The church here sure made a bad start! In the second century, the pseudonymous Epistle of Barnabas throughout disinherits Yisra'el. For instance, (alluding to Exodus 33:1-3) the Epistle manifests the idea that the church is the true heir of the promises in the תּוֹרָה Torah.[60]

Later in the second century, in 'The Letter to Diognetus' Levitical offerings are compared with idolatry; food laws and Sabbath keeping are 'superstitions' and 'utterly

---

59 Calvin Smith, editor, Maltz, chpt 1 in The Jews, Modern Israel and the New Supersessionism. For greater detail see Steve Maltz, How The Church Lost The Way, 2009, UK, pp. 23-68; How the Church Lost the Truth, 2010, UK, pp. 46-71; Hebraic Church, 2016, UK, pp. 19-24; Shalom, 2019, UK, pp. 25-33.

60 Diprose, Israel and the Church, pp. 69-73, 107-108.

ridiculous.' Depreciation of the Jews was extended to the תּוֹרָה Torah. The Bishop Irenaeus (178-195) is infamous for disinheriting Yisra'el of the promises of the תּוֹרָה Torah and endorsing the viewpoint that the church is the true Yisra'el. He read the תּוֹרָה Torah in the darkness of replacement theology. Tertullian (160-225) carried on in the same way – allegorising Scripture. Origen's (185-254) replacement theology went way beyond previous teaching. Whereas others before him read scripture literally and allegorically and the allegorical method before him was more in its infancy, Origen's development of the allegorical approach was to work out a complete hermeneutical theory. He was responsible for making allegory the main form of Bible interpretation for centuries to comes. Key themes of the תּוֹרָה Torah had to be re-evaluated. The theoretical basis of replacement theology he grounded into biblical exegesis. Basically he was ripping apart the Holy Jewish תּוֹרָה Torah. By using allegory, Origen, freely spiritualized the meaning of תּוֹרָה Torah passages where ethnic Israel is clearly intended while denigrating the Jewish people themselves. His allegoric work opened the door for cultural prejudice and an attitude of contempt toward Yisra'el. Where it was requested that יֵשׁוּעַ Yeshua be crucified and Barabbas be released, Origen suggests that Yisra'el has joined herself to another husband – 'Barabbas, the robber, the devil, while Christ has joined Himself to a new wife, the church. The 'lost sheep of Yisra'el' are the intelligent Gentiles who accept the gospel.[61] His contribution and version of replacement theology became a **standard position** in Christian theology for more than a thousand years [I can see it is still a standard position of many people

61 Calvin Smith, editor, Maltz, in The Jews, Modern Israel and the New Supersessionism, pp. 28-30; Diprose, Israel and the Church, pp. 81-85.

today]. Ambrose in 387 went further. Jews to him were perverse and incapable of any good thought. Jews were infidels, but words were not enough and anti-Semitism entrenched his thinking[62] to even endorse the burning of a Jewish synagogue.[63] Augustine (354-430) is believed to be the most influential theologian after the apostle Paul, affecting the history of every church doctrine. He shared the replacement theology of Origen and Ambrose and shared the anti-Semitism of Ambrose. In writing the 'Tract against the Jews', one of the most influential anti-Judaic writings from after the time of Origen, this tradition of replacement theology was made certain.[64]

After this, things now get much worse – the wheels of hatred are now greased. John Chrysostom (347-407), a popular church father, [65] left us with eight surviving sermons directed against the Jews. He wrote that the Jews were dogs, unfit for work but fit for killing and fit for slaughter. The synagogue is a brothel, a den of thieves, a lodging for wild beasts. Jews are abominable, lawless, murderous and enemies of God; he even lusted for combat

62 Diprose, Israel and the Church, p. 88.

63 See also Edward H. Flannery, The Anguish of the Jews, 1985 & 1999, USA, p. 60.

64 Diprose, Israel and the Church, p. 89.

65 Usually referred to as the Ante-Nicean Fathers, (the leaders of the primitive Christian Church up to 325 A.D.) - David Bivin and Roy Blizzard, Understanding the Difficult Words of Jesus, 1994, USA, p. 23. Any of about 70 theologians in the 2nd-7th century who established official church doctrine (Merril Bolender, When The Cross Became A Sword, 2012, USA, pp. 13 #2, 24-31); Al Garza, pp. 49-53; as many were pagan philosophers before conversion they also brought many pagan ideas into the church - Frank Viola and George Barna, Pagan Christianity, 2012, USA, pp. 91, 202.

against them.[66] These words titillated the ears for those disposed to the unnatural hatred of the Jews right up to today. He accused the Jews of murdering their children, of worshipping devils and with no opportunity for repentance for their role in the death of Christ. Since God hated them, Christians were also bound to utterly hate them as well. Jerome, born in 342, regarded as the most eloquent of the Latin church fathers, was also plainly committed to replacement theology and spread the lies that the synagogue was worse than a brothel, a den of vice, the devil's refuge, and satan's fortress. And adding fuel to the fire he said that there could never be expiation for the Jews as God had always hated them and therefore all Christians were to also hate them as they were the assassins of Christ and worshipped the devil.[67]

This general trend through the 'Adversus Judaeos' (anti-Judaic) literature produced an antagonism toward all things Jewish and further developed a theology of contempt. Cyril of Alexandria (370-444) is remembered because of his major input at the Council of Chalcedon. The anti-Semitism that drove him had now become the official position of the church. He went so far as to lead a pillage against the city's Jewish quarter – many Jews were killed and the rest were expelled from the city. Theological anti-Semitism also now found expression in state legislation, as seen with Pope Gregory 1 (540-604), spelling out certain rights and non-rights for the Jewish population. This gave legal warrant of mistrust toward the Jews facilitating the accusations and contempt by the Gentiles.

66 Calvin Smith, editor, Barry Horner, chpt 2 in The Jews, Modern Israel and the New Supersessionism, pp. 51-53

67 Diprose, Israel and the Church, pp. 89-91; Derek White, The Road to the Holocaust, Context (History), 1998, pp. 7-8.

Emperor Constantine in 325 wrote a letter to those bishops who were not present at the Council of Nicea concerning the date of Easter, he said, "We ought not, therefore, to have anything in common with the Jews." This attitude, that all things Jewish are incompatible with Christianity, shows what was behind subsequent legislation against the Jews. This concept was reflected in the confessions where Jews had to renounce their Jewishness to get baptised. So for the first time in history the church's theology concerning Israel formed **official policy** establishing a precedent for the making of official statements against the Jews. Constantine also "established a precedent for the practice of making official statements which discriminated from the Jews." As all things Jewish were anathema to Christianity, Easter and Christmas had to be given alternative dates (so why can't we as the church correct this, especially as we know that it was anti-Semitism that dictated the dates?[68]) Furthermore is the fact that it was Passover that was replaced by Easter, named after an old English goddess called *Eostre*, who already happened to have a feast in her honour at that time of the year. Easter, as well as the Sabbath, would now be totally independent from the Jewish calendar. These biblical events have 'been stripped from their context and applied according to the whims of the rulers of the established church. God just did not have a say in it...'[69]

---

68 With all the Jewish literature I have, I have not ran into any that would disagree that Yeshua was born during the Feast of Tabernacles – October in the Jewish calender, (as he tabernacled with us). The Hebrew calender and the biblical feasts have all been totally sabotaged by the early church. But it needs reminding that some of these dates and feasts are applied even to Gentiles now and in the 1000 year reign! Even Maltz agrees that it is not to late to revive the meaning of the feasts and appropriate dates. See Hebraic Church, pp. 140-144.

69 Steve Maltz, Shalom, pp. 121-125.

The Synod of Antioch (341) stated that "whoever observes Easter at the same time as the Jews makes himself 'alien from the church, as one who not only heaps sins on himself, but who is also the cause of destruction and subversion of many.'" The Synod of Laodicea further legislated against observing Jewish festivals when Jews do, as Christians were no longer allowed to receive portions sent from their feasts including unleavened bread, or to feast with the them. The legal rights of the Jews were greatly restricted by 'The Code of Canons of the African Church' (419 and issued by 217 'fathers') which stated that heretics and the heathen (the Jews) now were no longer permitted to bring legal accusations against the non-Jews. The Council of Chalcedon added "that no Christian parent was to give his child in marriage to a Jew."[70] At Toledo (631) it was determined what punishments would be enforced for Jews who had received Christian baptism but later lapsed on it. Some of the punishments were very severe such as taking children away from the parents. In a mixed marriage a choice had to be made of separation or accepting 'Christianity.' Jews who rejected baptism could not hold office and were deprived of their children. At Trullo (692) it was forbidden to eat unleavened bread of the Jews, nor anything to do with them, nor receive their help when sick or to receive medicine from them etc. – the penalty being 'deposed' or 'cut off.' Clergymen and laymen were no longer allowed to enter a synagogue to pray; if caught they were excommunicated. Then came the seventh 'ecumenical' council (11 Nicea, 787) where it was stipulated that Jewish converts abandon all semblances of their custom/ordinances. In other words – Jews were being

70 Diprose, Israel and the Church, pp. 93-94, 126-127.

denied the privileges of citizenship, living in a social/legal ghetto, which we will see, eventually materialized.[71]

Further down this slippery slope, as things got worse, we have the 4th Lateran Council (1215). Furthering previous defamation of the Jews, Crusaders were no longer required to pay debts to Jewish lenders. Curtailing commerce with Jews, denying them public functions and stopping their appearance in public during Holy Week – and what was even worse imposed on them, was the distinctive clothing or badge to mark them. Now the Jew had no safe place to go! These anti-Semitic canons, it must be emphasised, were formulated by church 'Councils'. There is no question that the underlying problem with the church was replacement theology, which in turn relied on allegory to interpret scripture.[72] It also clearly shows that by now the church was anti-Semitic. In Diprose's words,

> Replacement theology and it's corollary – the Church's self-understanding as the true Israel – are historically linked with overt **contempt** for Israel. This is evident both in the 'Adversus Judaeous' tradition and the anti-Semitic thought and practice of Post-Reformation Europe.[73]

> Don't delude yourselves: no one makes a fool of God! A person reaps what he sows.[74]

> Rather, each person is being tempted whenever he is being dragged off and enticed by the bait of his

71 Ibid., pp. 94-95.
72 Ibid., pp. 95-97.
73 Diprose, Israel and the Church, p. 134, emphasis mine.
74 Galatians 6:7.

> own desire. Then, having conceived, the desire gives birth to sin; and when sin is fully grown, it gives birth to death.[75]

Theology has consequences. These two verses remind us that when one embraces bad theology there will be negative output. It forms our world-and-life-view. Our world-and-life-view forms our attitudes and dictates how we live out our life; in what we do practically. Replacement theology put into action caused the death of many Jews – and this is where we now turn. I am again only presenting a skeletal history.

The Living out of anti-Semitism

Colin Barnes wrote,

> Hard (or punitive) supersessionism especially carries within it a clear theological understanding of the Jewish people. It states that the covenants God made with the Jews were invalidated by Jewish unfaithfulness, and therefore, ...those covenants now belong to the Church. These doctrines were taught and strengthened by reference both to Jewish wickedness (Jews being the 'Children of Judas', etc.) and to Jewish misery. Jewish wickedness proved that God was just in taking the covenants from them, while Jewish suffering proved that they were indeed under his judgement. This triumphalist version of supersessionism is therefore predisposed to anti-

75 James 1:14-15.

> Semitism, as evidenced throughout much of the Church's history.[76]

Clark Williamson on the same note writes,

> The Church's theological understanding of itself in relation to Jews and Judaism was never mere theorizing. Theory, interpretation, always has a practical moment. The Church's anti-Judaism reflects and reinforces anti-Jewish practice, whether that practice is internal to the Church in how it talks about Jews and Judaism and itself, in the ideas and attitudes that people adopt toward Jews, or whether it finds its ramifications in more visible and public forms, such as legislation or a willingness to tolerate violence or discrimination against Jews.[77]

Replacement theology affirms the idea that the church has replaced Yisra'el and the Jews in the purposes of God.

> It views Christianity and indeed [Yeshua] himself as the fulfilment of all things Jewish and Old Testament. It carries with it significant implications for the way the present state, land and people of [Yisra'el] are viewed, but essentially undermines the clear teaching of scripture.[78]

---

76 Calvin Smith, editor, Colin Barnes, chpt 3 in The Jews, Modern Israel and the New Supersessionism, p. 65. There are 3 forms identified – punitive, economic and structural, p. 168 (Two camps are identified by Revd Frank Andrews, Is There Death in the Pot, p. 8.)

77 Clark Williamson as cited by Colin Barnes, Ibid., p. 66.

78 Reuben Gardiner, Prayer for Israel, Autumn magazine 2018, p. 12.

It is a theology that divests Yisra'el of its national, ethnic or territorial identity or destiny as there are no promises that remain for the Jewish people on a national level.[79] Ilse Posselt puts it this way,

> At its core, supersessionism therefore nullifies God's covenant promises to the descendants of Abraham, Isaac and Jacob, removing from them all the blessings – yet not the curses – offered in the [תּוֹרָה Torah] and placing them upon God's spiritual Israel, the church, which now supersedes ethnic and historical Israel.[80]

Such triumphalist supersessionism and the continued demonisation of the Jew brought things to the point where the collaboration or acquiescence of the European churches made possible the horrors of the holocaust.[81]

> According to Eckardt, 'The primary agent in western anti-Semitism is the Christian message and the Christian church ... [this] has become a truism of historical, psychological and theological scholarship.' As Hay commented, 'Hatred was the product of clerical propaganda.'[82]

James Carroll, referring to anti-Semitic sermons, says,

---

79 Kesher Web.com, YouTube, Anti-Semitism – Covenant & Controversy, part 1, The Great Rage.

80 The Jerusalem Post, October 2016, p. 26. See also Darrell l. Block, Mitch Glaser, editors, Israel the Church and the Middle East, 2018, USA, pp. 104-106, 121.

81 Calvin Smith, Colin Barnes, chpt 3 in The Jews, Modern Israel and the New Supersessionism, pp. 67-68.

82 Eckardt and Hay as cited by Colin Barnes, Ibid., p. 66.

> Such words inevitably led to actions: assaults on synagogues, the exclusion of Jews from public office, expulsions… Should we be surprised that not long after these sermons were preached, there were several violent outbursts against Jews in Antioch?[83]

Flannery concurs,

> Of more immediate import to the fate of the Jews than the opinions of the apologists and theologians of the patristic era were the legislative measures taken by both the Church and the empire. In a sense these were the translation into statutory form of what the patristic teaching seemed to call for. Some anti-Jewish legislation by the Church could be anticipated. As long as fraternizing among Christians and Jews and Judaizing among Christians were strong it is not surprising that counter-measures found their way into the canons of the Church councils.[84]

This illustrates the fact that the Question of Yisra'el and the Jews are rarely neutral and responses often reveal our motivation.[85]

In Spain the council of Elvira (306) forbade Jewish-Christian marriage and banned close relations between Jewish-Christian communities etc.. The Council of Antioch

---

83 James Carroll as cited by Colin Barnes, Ibid., pp. 52-53.
84 Flannery, The Anguish of the Jews, p. 55.
85 Prayer for Israel, Autumn magazine 2018, p. 13.

(341) prohibited Christians to celebrate Passover with the Jews. The Council of Laodicea (434-481) forbade Christians from keeping the Jewish Sabbath or to receive gifts or unleavened bread from festivals.[86] Construction and the care of synagogues were put under regulation. In 423, it was forbidden to beautify or repair them without permission. The civil status of the Jew changed – they were barred from public functions (army, administrative posts, legal professions etc.). Marrying the Jew now brought the death penalty. Jewish tribunals were invalidated in matters not purely religious. Judaism was said to be the 'wicked sect'; Jews were abominable.[87]

Hostilities grew, becoming brutal and frequent. For example, in Alexandria (414) there was a Jewish uprising where many Jews were killed. In Italy a Bishop encouraged a synagogue to be destroyed to be replaced by a church and a similar instance of this occurred in Africa. In Rome a synagogue was destroyed. In Edessa a synagogue was taken. In Minorca, a synagogue was burned down. In the land of Yisra'el, a group of monks attacked a synagogue and murdered Jews.[88]

By the mid 5th century,

> the transformation of the Jewish status was complete. The struggle with the Church was lost, and Hellenistic trends in Judaism were defunct. The national and cultural center was now in Babylonia, and the patriarchate was gone. In the eyes of the

86 Flannery, p. 55.
87 Ibid., p. 57.
88 Ibid., pp. 59-60.

> Church, the Jew was a guilt-laden unbeliever resistant to grace and a destroyer of souls.[89]

To the Empire a Jew was just tolerated as a second-class citizen. Theological negation and polemical intensity produced "an effect that is no longer purely theological or polemical: ideological opposition has turned to hatred and stereotype – the life blood of anti-semitism." Judaism was no longer God's vessel of salvation and was replaced by the church with the view that the Jew was wicked and despicable, unworthy and rejected. Jews were not only wrong but evil.[90] After the 430's, things got worse. During the reign of Emperor Zeno (474-491) there were massacres and when a synagogue was burned including bones of the dead, the Emperor remarked that it "would have been better to burn live Jews instead." Under Anastatius 1 (430-518), Jews were murdered and synagogues burned. John of Ephesus (516-585) converted seven synagogues into churches. Justinian 1 (483-565) eliminated many Jewish rights including barring Jews from public functions, practising law and their prevention from testifying against a Christian. Since he considered himself to be Emperor, he wanted to see that Judaism functioned 'properly.' For example, the synagogue must not celebrate the Passover before the Christian Easter. The **תּוֹרָה** Torah should not be read in Hebrew. Those who believed in the last judgement or in angels were to be excommunicated and put to death. This led to abuses of course – in Borion, North Africa (535), Jews were outlawed, synagogues closed and forced baptisms were done. Many Jews died in those days and were eventually banished from Yerushalayim in 634.

89 Ibid., p. 61.

90 Ibid., pp. 62-63.

Things got so bad that later when the Islamic armies arrived, the Jews welcomed them. [91] (How ironic when one considers eschatology comprising an Islamic anti-christ and a Jewish Messiah, Yeshua Hamashiach).

In Spain the Jews also were forbidden to marry Christians or hold public office. But under King Sisebut (612-621), Jews had to receive baptism or be exiled. In 636 it was ruled that those who were baptised were to avoid relations with unbaptised Jews;

> in cases where the children of unbaptised Jews had been baptised, the children were to be taken from them for Christian education.
>
> This last decision opened another sad chapter in the history of Christendom. The removal of children from their non-Christian parents occurred many times throughout Church history and found examples up to the nineteenth and twentieth centuries…

In 636, Chintila kicked out all Jews from his kingdom and in Toledo it was also imposed that all future kings, under the threat of eternal fire, do the same. Recceswinth (649-672) imposed humiliating punishments of flogging and hair extraction, in other words they were tortured. Violators were burned or stoned and Christians were even forbidden to help. These were the conditions till the Muslims overran Spain in 711.[92]

---

91 Ibid., pp. 67-70.
92 Ibid., pp.75-77.

The Crusades[93] began in 1096. Nobles, knights, monks and peasants (they were also rapists, thieves, and robbers whose sins were forgiven by the pope in advance[94]) turned on the Jews in a frenzy killing one quarter to one third of the Jewish population in Germany and France (around 10,000). Flannery remarked that "strangely, in the wake of the massacres, popular hostility toward Jews increased and their social position suffered further deterioration. A vague assumption that the atrocities must have been deserved took possession of the suggestible popular mind." The second Crusade (1146) experienced the same miseries.[95]

By the end of the 13th century, the Jews were expelled from England (1290), then France, and most of Germany. Contributing to the destruction of the Jew were baseless accusations like the 'ritual murder libel' or 'blood accusation' (the murder of a Christian for religious purposes). These profoundly stupid accusations rang into the itching ears of 'Christians' century after century – leaving a stream of Jewish blood. As late as the 20th century these libels prevailed in some countries! So when a dead person was found – Jews paid the price, often by being burnt alive.[96]

As mentioned before, there was the evil and injurious action of forcing one to wear distinctive clothes or a 'badge of shame'. France was the first to introduce it. Eventually it

---

93 Any of the military expeditions undertaken by Christian powers in the 11th-13th centuries to win the Holy Land from the Muslims. But Muslims and Jews were targets as they were both heretics and imposters. Merril Bolender, When The Cross Became A Sword, p. 9.

94 John Hagee, Jerusalem Countdown, 2006, USA, p. 66.

95 Flannery, pp. 91, 93.

96 Ibid., pp. 98-100.

took on many forms, for instance, the Jewish hat in Germany; the pointed hat in Poland. In Sicily, Jewish shops were marked by a circle. To the Jew all this was noxious, an insult, and it marked them off as a target of violence causing many to lose self-respect, and to become careless in speech and dress. Unsurprisingly this nourished a resentment of his oppressors.[97] In Germany and Austria (1298) about 100,000 Jews perished. Things even got worse in the 14th century as Jews were being blamed for every small or great evil. Soon Jewish history in France came to an end. In 1306 all Jews were arrested on a single day and expelled from the country but nine years later were invited back, as they were needed for the economy. Instead of being thankful they were repaid in 1320 with a crusade of 40,000 hoodlums who wiped out over 120 Jewish communities.[98]

In the years 1348-1350 a systematic holocaust took place all over Europe. Jews were assigned to torture and then the flames. For example, in Strassburg,[99] 2000 were burned and for good reason from the perpetrator's perspective, as this action guaranteed their sins would be forgiven. Any survivors were expelled in 1386. Over 200 communities were destroyed. In Germany expulsions continued to the end of the 15 century.[100] Arrests, pogroms,[101] confiscations, expulsions, prison etc. continued in Europe. In 1492 Jews were expelled from Spain – all 300,000 of them only to

97 Ibid., pp. 103-104.

98 Ibid., pp. 107-108.

99 Ibid., p. 112.

100 The multiple expulsions were because Germany was decentralized, so often Jews just moved from one area to another.

101 An organized, often officially encouraged massacre or persecution of a minority group but especially for the Jew (Merril Bolender, p. 9).

further face shipwreck, piracy, starvation, and slavery. Many made it to Spain only to face the Inquisition[102] (they were actually torture chambers[103]) which was set up to find Jews that didn't really 'Christianize.' It was utterly ruthless and a terror for all Jews, and lasted until the 20th century![104]

In England, King John (1167-1216) imprisoned all Jews and tortured many. Henry III (1207-1272) taxed the Jews to the point that they were unable to pay, so they tried in vain to leave England but were unable to do so. In 1222, the wicked and despicable badge was enforced and it was illegal to sell food to the Jew. In 1225 a Christian child was found dead resulting in 90 Jews sent to prison and 18 executed.[105] It is indeed interesting how such hatred can consume us; executing 18 people and imprisoning 90 others for the death of one child – that probably had nothing to do with the Jew in the first place. It seems to me that replacement theology giving birth to anti-Semitism invites the demons to incite us. So called 'Christians' embraced an anti-Jewish worldview which fostered their evil natures. It certainly makes one wonder how small in number genuine believers were and are?

Instead of one made in the image of God and the people group that brought us the **תּוֹרָה** Torah, Flannery writes,

102 A Roman Catholic tribunal for discovery and punishment of heresy of the Jews and was instituted by Pope Innocent 111 (1198-1216) in Rome (Merril Bolender, p. 9).

103 Hagee, p. 75; Mike Evans, Jew-Hatred and the Church, 2016, USA, pp. 213-214.

104 Flannery, pp. 109-140.

105 Ibid., pp. 119-121.

> Of grave significance was the utter deterioration of the Jewish image in the late Middle ages. The dissociation of the imaginary from the real Jew effected earlier under theological influence was now complete. The terms 'Jewish' and 'diabolical' had become all but synonymous. The deliberate unbeliever and blasphemer was now also ritual murderer and poisoner of mankind, arch-conspirator, oppressor of the poor, sorcerer and magician; in short, the agent of Satan. Medieval art gave plentiful evidence of the figure: Invariably, the Jew was portrayed with horns, a tail, an evil visage; his company is that of devils, sows, scorpions, and his poses grotesque. [106]

The 16th-18th centuries were the age of the ghetto, a place usually enclosed by high walls, guarded gates, and paid for by those inside! Most were overcrowded and there was the fear of frequent plagues and fire. Though massacres were now rare, the image of the Jew deteriorated. And more than anywhere else, anti-Semitism flourished in France and England. These were now Jew-less lands, but 'where the Jew did not exist, he was invented'. Anti-Jewish material was everywhere, in catechisms, sermons, and writings. The foremost preacher at the time, Bossuet (1627-1704), in France accused the Jews as an accursed race, haters of God, now scattered in all countries and a laughing stock. Though anti-Semitism was endemic, Jews were let back in but 'by the back door'. Even a humanist could proclaim, "If it is Christian to hate Jews, then we are all good Christians." This brought on some savage attacks to the ghettos and further expulsions. In 1670, the Jews were forced to leave

---

106 Ibid., p. 143.

Vienna and were ordered to leave Bohemia in 1747 (but the Jews remained following the intercession of Hofjuden, court Jews, with European royalty who then interceded with Maria Theresa).[107]

There is one person who fanned the flames more than any other; his name is Martin Luther (1483-1546). Though pre-eminent in the Reformation and lauded by evangelicals, Frank Andrews said that he became one of the leading advocates of replacement theology. He promoted anti-Jewishness to a "level not seen before in Europe." Luther

> went so far as to suggest that Christians would not be at fault in God's sight for killing Jews since the Jews were guilty of killing [Yeshua]. At this point Luther did not even suggest that Jews which had converted to Christianity should be exempt from this process. At this stage in life he had reached the conclusion that Jews were not even worth converting.[108]

He raged at them, as Flannery voices well,

> … he raged at them in a language that at least equalled in violence anything uttered against them before or after. With biting sarcasm and occasional scatological insult, he renewed all the old charges of the past: Jews are poisoners, ritual murderers, usurers; they are parasites on Christian society; they are worse than devils; it is harder to convert them

107 Ibid., pp. 145-153.

108 Revd Frank Andrews, Is There Death in the Pot, pp. 51, 63. This influence of replacement theology is still installed through the UK's seminaries and colleges (p. 68).

> than Satan himself; they are doomed to hell. They are, in truth, the anti-Christ. Their synagogues should be destroyed and their books seized; they should be forced to work with their hand; better still they should be expelled by the princes from their territories. … In his last sermon, delivered a few days before his death, he called urgently for their expulsion from all Germany. The devil the reformer would have exorcised from the Church seemed to have taken full possession of him.[109]

And Hitler did just that. And from what Europe had already done to the Jew, it is clear Hitler did what Europe desired to do but didn't accomplish. Flannery continues, in Poland (1648-1658) between 100,000-500,000 Jews were murdered. Except for the Nazi period, in the 16th-18th centuries **anti-Semitism had come to full fruition,** and its bitter fruits were devastating.[110]

During the interim between WW1 and 2, Germany suffered extreme unrest and humiliation by the loss of war. Many looked for some face-saving reason for Germany's misfortune. It was easy to find – the Jew of course![111] In a periodical (1935) for Catholic Priests, it 'exposed' the role of Jews in the German defeat. The Protestant churches of Thuringia, Saxony, Nassau-Hesse, Schleswig-Holstein, Anstalt, and Lubeck publicly wrote that they believed that the Jews were the cause of the war and stood with those who would take action against the Jews. These, Colin Barnes stresses,

---

109 Flannery, pp. 152-153.
110 Flannery, pp. 157-159, emphasis mine.
111 Ibid., p. 206.

> were the direct results of the churches' own doctrinal positions. The Jew was the traitor. Jerome for instance, writing in his Homily on Psalm 108, had stated that; 'the Jews take their name, not from Judah who was a holy man, but from the betrayer. From the former we (Christians) are spiritual Jews, from the traitor come the carnal Jews.' This was supersessionism in practice. The Jews were traitors according to the doctrines of the church, and the church acted upon and propagated those doctrines. In all this, the churches and the Nazi Party drew disturbingly close. Indeed, after viewing the three hundredth anniversary performance of the Oberammergau Passion Play in 1934, Hitler praised it as 'a precious tool' in the war against the Jews.

This set up the anti-Jewish mindset which "contributed to, and even legitimised, Nazi Germany's Jewish policy."

> In the years leading to and during the Holocaust, the churches across Europe, for their own theological reasons and doctrines, as said before, continued to demonise the Jews to the point where collaboration with the Nazis was possible.

At one point, 70-80% of Protestant pastors were members of the German National People's Party.[112] Some of the 14 senior members of the Nazi party at the January 20 1942 'Final Solution' conference in Berlin were Protestant

---

112 Calvin Smith, editor, Colin Barnes, chpt 3 in The Jews, Modern Israel and the New Supersessionism, pp. 67-69.

ministers![113] Andrews adds, "The Protestant church in Germany hosted Hitler in 1924 and applauded him when he promised to get rid of the Jews."[114] It therefore should not surprise anyone that no church in Germany objected to Hitler's discriminating laws against the Jews. Already for 1700 years the church had fully approved restrictive laws for the Jews. So when deportations started, no protest was heard because 'that was what was supposed to happen to Jews'.[115] Just to note that the Bulgarian Church prevented 50,000 Jews from being sent to death camps – a rare example of true Christianity.

And for Hitler, Flannery observes, "The one catalyst that above all else enabled him to reconcile oppositions and finally transform Germany from a liberal republic into a totalitarian state in a single decade was his anti-Semitism." Hitler's anti-Semitism was more intense though; it was nihilistic, boundless in fury, the Jew was the epitome of evil. This actually appealed to all sections of German society. Hitler swayed the 'Christians' in his *Mein Kampf* saying, "I believe that I am today acting in accordance with the will of the Almighty Creator: by defending myself against the Jew I am fighting for the work of the Lord."[116]

Hitler loved Luther's theology and quoted him as did Friedrich Nietzsche. He even stated that in honour of Luther's birthday he would launch the first large-scale Nazi pogrom. Indeed Hitler felt 'unrestricted acceptance of

113 David Soakwell, In Touch mag., (Christian Friends of Israel), 1st Quarter 2019, No 198, pp. 5-6.
114 Revd Frank Andrews, Is There Death in the Pot, p. 75.
115 Ibid., pp. 72, 75, 78.
116 Flannery, pp. 209-210.

national socialism by the Vatican'.[117] The entire world knew what the Nazis were up to so in 1938 the League of Nations (forerunner of the United Nations), held a conference in Évian, France to formulate a plan to rescue the Jews of Europe, but with many deliberations, adopted a nearly unanimous plan **to do absolutely nothing.**[118] When Hitler saw that other nations, including the USA, were refusing the entry of the Jews, considered that he had been given the green light to carry out the result of almost 2000 years of replacement theology and anti-Semitism.[119] So Hitler could legitimately say to Cardinal Faulhaber, "I am only doing what the Church itself has been teaching and practising against the Jews." The conversation was repeated with Bishop Berning and Berlin's Vicar-General (1933) before the signing of the Concordate between the Vatican and the Third Reich where upon Hitler gave himself the recognition of himself being a catholic.[120]

The Obvious Reason for the Name 'Jesus'

This survey of replacement theology and anti-Semitism could have been much shorter (or longer of course) but I wanted to engrave on our minds and hearts the severity of the situation of erroneous theology and anti-Semitism. Remember on page 12 where I said (concerning how Yeshua became Jesus), "Unfortunately the ee sound remained as later English speakers **wrongly interpreted** that **יֵשׁוּעַ** Yeshua began with the ee sound instead of the 'Yeh'." Well it doesn't take a lot of intellect to find out how

117 John Hagee, pp. 78-80; Mike Evans, p. 258.
118 Nehemia Gordon and Keith Johnson, p. 166.
119 Evans, pp. 263, 277; Derek White, The Road to the Holocaust, pp. 20.
120 Derek White, p. 21.

to say 'Yeshua' does it? However, our anti-Semitic forefathers were intent on disallowing any attachment to any Jewish reference. In the Common Prayer Hymns A&M, first published in 1549 but had a major revision in 1662, (the copy I have, had to have been printed after 1953[121]), still used the name Jesu and Jesus. I find this remarkable. For at least any American or European, linguistically it would have been very easy to transition from Jesu, (which at least at some prior date than 1953 the 'J' was pronounced as Ye), to Yeshua. The leaders of the church could not have been so ignorant or have been prevented to know the Hebrew name יֵשׁוּעַ Yeshua, after all there were approximately a quarter of a million Jews who had put their faith in יֵשׁוּעַ Yeshua living throughout Europe and England at that time.[122] But I deem it is obvious why they could not permit the name יֵשׁוּעַ Yeshua. I suggest it was due to the hostile climate of replacement theology and anti-Semitism. A Jewish name for our Saviour, for the Gentile Christian especially at that time, would have been unthinkable, anathema, intolerable. The church replaced the 'horrid' Jew and Judaism, so naturally the only 'proper' name for God's Son would be 'Jesus,' a name with no particular meaning, with a perfect non-Jewish ring to it.

Going back to Lex Meyers' statement: Some people

> claim that His name was changed to Jesus to hide the fact that He was a Jew, since Jesus is based on a Greek name rather than a Hebrew name. **While it is possible that there might be some truth to this claim**, [where I agree with Meyers but not just *some*

121 It does not have a published date in it.

122 John Fischer, How Jewish is Christianity?, 2003, USA, p. 51.

> truth] it is far fetched to think that it was some grand conspiracy to hide the Jewishness of Jesus, since the Bible clearly says that He was a Jew.[123]

He is right when he says that the Bible clearly says that He was a Jew. At least the leaders of the church after the invention of printing press (1450), should have had copies of the Scriptures. But, remember when I wrote that in the 16th-18th centuries anti-Semitism had come to **full fruition**; and that will not have changed right up to the holocaust. Nowhere does the Bible proffer a view that would support the notion of replacement theology and its venomous anti-Semitism (both are incomprehensible and incompatible with the complete **תּוֹרָה** Torah). But this did not prevent church leaders steeped in their theological anti-Semitism, ignorant of Scripture, wilfully preventing the name **יֵשׁוּעַ** Yeshua to get off the ground. Rav Sha'ul, author of over 20 books, agrees, saying that it was **intentional** not to use **יֵשׁוּעַ** Yeshua![124]

Meyer also asked,

> If Joshua and Jesus share the same Hebrew and Greek names, why are they given different English names? Some people assume there is a great conspiracy involved in why the names are different, however, it is a very simple reason. When the Old Testament Hebrew text was translated into English, they phonetically translated 'Yeshua' as 'Joshua,' and when they translated the Greek New Testament into English, they phonetically translated 'Iesous'

123 Page 13-14 of this writing.
124 The Yahushaic Covenant, vol. 1, pp. 67, 88, 95, 161.

as 'Jesus', with one exception, when 'Iesous' referred to Joshua son of Nun the translators chose to continue using the name Joshua to avoid confusion.[125]

The problem with this excuse is that the dilemma was very easily rectified by using the name 'Joshua the son of Nun' when necessary. In the תּוֹרָה Torah it is common to state the first name of someone and then name his father. In the R.C. there are various 'Marys', but usually it is specified which Mary they are referring to (John 19:25, 20:1). There are two people named Judah in the R.C., one being Judah Iscariot and the other Judah Thaddeus. יֵשׁוּעַ Yeshua was also referred to as יֵשׁוּעַ מְנָצְרִי (Yeshua the Nazarene) which was how He was actually known as (Matthew 2:23, John 18:5,7) or יֵשׁוּעַ בֶּן יוֹסֵף (Yeshua son of Yosef).[126] He was also known as רַבִּי Rabbi (John 3:2, 4:31, 6:25, 20:16) so could רַבִּי יֵשׁוּעַ Rabbi Yeshua been a good option? They could have also used the name יֵשׁוּעַ הַמָּשִׁיחַ Yeshua Hamashiach (Yeshua the Messiah). Another way a translator could have solved the problem was the way they differentiated between the names יְהֹוָה Yehovah and Adonai – capitals were used printing the word LORD (Yehovah) and non-capitals for Lord (Adonai). So was this a conspiracy in giving Joshua his name but not Yeshua? Most certainly it was. At the least it was extremely poor judgement, very poor indeed. Rav Sha'ul calls it 'a gross mis-handling of the Messiah's name at best...'[127] But I am inclined to a 'great conspiracy' involving the top/high-up

---

125 Lex Meyer, How Yeshua became Jesus, http://unlearnthelies.com/how-yeshua-became-jesus.html

126 See also Lois Goldberg, How Jewish is Christianity?, p. 15.

127 Ibid., p. 106.

leaders; those of great influence and or power. If we add that it was ultimately satan himself who blinded their eyes to have the Jews/Judaism demonised and replaced by the church it was natural to prevent the proclamation of the Jewish Messiah יֵשׁוּעַ Yeshua.[128]

Steve Maltz made an interesting comment relating to this.

> ...isn't it strange that the [R.C.] name 'James' is exactly the same as the [Tanach] name, 'Jacob'. Both are translations [I, Leo am sure he meant transliterations] of the Hebrew name Ya'acov, yet one sounds very Jewish and the other very British. Perhaps the reason why the [R.C.] translators used the *British* name was in some way to distance Christians from the Jewish Old Testament, reinforcing the idea (actually a feature of ancient heresy, Marcionism) that the [Tanach] is out-of-date, somehow lesser among equals (though of course another reason was to keep King James – he of the KJV – happy).[129]

Maltz has a point but I think it goes much farther than this. Stern has something interesting to add to all this as he points out that a vicious circle of Christian anti-Semitism feeds on the Renewed Covenant. The R.C. within itself has no anti-Semitism, but anti-Semitism has misused the R.C. to justify

---

128 Maltz spells out the root cause of anti-Semitism which vindicates my above thesis. The answer is "Messiah." The Jews were the target of the Satan, not only to stop the Messiah from being born, but because of His return. For this to happen the Jews must be in their land and in a position to say "Blessed is he who comes in the name of the Lord." Steve Maltz, How The Church Lost The Way, p. 165.

129 Steve Maltz, To Life!, 2011, UK, p. 59.

itself and influence Christian Theology. Translators, steeped in that anti-Semitism, produce anti-Semitic translations (even if not intentionally anti-Jewish). These absorbed attitudes, alien to Judaism, influence the reader. They may in turn become theologians/preachers perpetuating this dark anti-Semitic character, and refining and developing the anti-Semitic side of theology (even if unaware of the anti-Semitism). Others, we know, act out this anti-Semitism persecuting the Jews and may even think this serves God. This vicious circle must be broken.[130] This is why it is so important that those who are blessed by the Lord in seeing through Christian anti-Semitism make an effort to inform, reprove and teach our brethren the Hebraic roots of our faith.

The Bible expresses that there is much deceit and wickedness, especially in high places. Conspiracies abound! The **תּוֹרָה** Torah says, "...those who hate you are raising their heads, craftily conspiring against your people…;" and "why did the nations rage and the peoples devise useless plans? The kings of the earth took their stand; and the rulers assembled together against **יְהֹוָה** Yehovah **and against his Messiah**."[131] Notice, and against his Messiah ie. **יֵשׁוּעַ** Yeshua. These verses teach that in this world we should expect conspiracies. Where evil abounds, so conspiracies abound. Therefore I believe Meyer is wrong when he cannot imagine a conspiracy behind the name 'Jesus'.

I am fully convinced that a conspiracy loaded with contempt for the Jew did take place in choosing the name 'Jesus' over **יֵשׁוּעַ** Yeshua. As satan wanted to destroy the

---

130 Stern, The Complete Jewish Study Bible, pp. xlv-xlvi.
131 Psalm 83:4 (3) and Acts 4:25-27.

church and the Jews, and blot out the name of Yeshua (below we will see why satan wanted to erase the name of יֵשׁוּעַ Yeshua from our minds), the name 'Jesus' served satan well – produced by replacement theology and anti-Semitism – only in the name of 'Jesus' could 'Christians' sing hymns[132] while Jews were being burnt alive, and using Scripture to validate it,[133] bringing condemnation on those 'Christians' at the same time and making it almost impossible for the Jew then to know the true יֵשׁוּעַ Yeshua. On the name 'Jesus' Merril Bolender, in her words writes, "There is nothing more repelling and repugnant to the Jew than the name Christ, because in that name they were historically persecuted, driven out, hunted down, and burned at the stake."[134] In Rabbi Abraham Heschel's words, (he escaped from the Nazis but his mother and two of his sisters perished in the concentration camps)

> If I should go to Poland or Germany, every stone, every tree would remind me of **contempt**, hatred, murder, of children killed, of mothers burned alive, of human beings asphyxiated.[135]

I know this is extremely harsh but I do not believe in the god of the Gentiles, 'Jesus,' I believe in יֵשׁוּעַ Yeshua the God of the Jews and non-Jews. As the name 'Jesus' comes

---

132 When Crusaders took control of Palestine, the Jews that gathered in the synagogue in Jerusalem were burnt to death as Crusaders sang the hymn 'O Christ we adore thee.' Revd Frank Andrews, Is There Death in the Pot, p. 71.

133 Evans, p. 190; From Jn 15:6 – 'If a man abide not abide in me, he is cast forth as a branch, and is withered; and men gather them, and cast them into the fire, and they are burned.' p. 195 and Hagee, p. 74.

134 Merril Bolender, When The Cross Became A Sword, p. 66.

135 Rabbi Abraham Heschel's as quoted by Steve Maltz, Hebraic Church, p. 120, emphasis mine.

out of the spirit of anti-Semitism, the name to me represents the antagonism to the Jew and to יֵשׁוּעַ Yeshua Himself. The name to me now sounds horrible, it hurts my ears especially now that I know the history behind it. The name to me is pagan. It expresses the haughtiness of the church and the church's unwillingness to learn from and submit to Judaism or to The King of the Jews. The name 'Jesus' takes us away from who יֵשׁוּעַ Yeshua really is.[136]

One of the most important discoveries concerning The Name is that יֵשׁוּעַ Yeshua is found in the First Covenant twenty eight times! It is transliterated as 'Jeshua.'[137] Only a conspiracy or utter contempt for truth could allow the First Covenant יֵשׁוּעַ, full of meaning, to be called 'Jeshua' and the R.C. יֵשׁוּעַ Yeshua to be called 'Jesus,' a name with no meaning!

I think the point is clear – we need to replace the name 'Jesus', when using the Son of God's name, to using His true name יֵשׁוּעַ Yeshua, the God who saves. People obviously can kill Jews in the name of 'Jesus' but I am convinced (as the history of the conceiving of the name 'Jesus' I think vindicates me) they could not have killed the Jews in the name of יֵשׁוּעַ Yeshua. If the church kept the name יֵשׁוּעַ Yeshua that would have presupposed the retention of the church's true spiritual Hebrew/Jewish roots and its theology, preventing the growth of replacement

---

136 Steve Maltz asks the question, "Which Jesus do you follow?" His question is in relation to if you follow the Greek perception of Yeshua or the Hebrew perception. His question could also be used in relation to the issues I have brought up concerning Yeshua. To Life, pp. 152-160.

137 Lois Tverberg, Walking in the Dust of Rabbi Jesus, p. 207; Rabbi Tuly Weisz, The Israel Bible, 2018, Koren Publishers Jerusalem, (Israel365), p. 2167.

theology in the first place. There never was meaning in the name 'Jesus' and never will be. An angel declared his name, (we now clearly see in the more original Hebrew Matthew manuscripts) 2000 years ago, and **that is the name we were commanded to call him!** Sometimes **יֵשׁוּעַ** Yeshua's name became part of His message. In Luke 19:1-10, Rabbi **יֵשׁוּעַ** seeing Zakkai called him to come down, declaring that He had to stay at his house that day. Zakkai acted in repentance of his past and **יֵשׁוּעַ** Yeshua said to him, 'Today **תְּשׁוּעָה** (teshua) salvation has come to this house...'[138] As we are taught that **יֵשׁוּעַ** Yeshua is the whole focal point of the Bible, surely we can get at least His name right? Also we need to say **יֵשׁוּעַ** Yeshua to retain the connection to the abbreviated form of **יְהוֹשֻׁעַ** Yehoshua (Joshua) as these two names both mean '**יְהֹוָה** Yehovah saves.'[139] In using The Name, Mel Gibson gave us a head start in the film 'The Passion of Christ' where His real name was used. Thank you Mel as 10's of millions around the world heard The Name **יֵשׁוּעַ** Yeshua for the first time![140]

The Importance of a Name

Years ago, at a 'Jewish' conference I attended, at some point when we were in small groups, someone said something that produced a reaction from a young Jewish girl. Someone asked her what she thought of the name 'Jesus'. I remember her reaction – taken aback, repulsed at

138 Lois Tverberg, Walking in the Dust of Rabbi Jesus, pp. 83-84.

139 Nehemia Gordon and Keith Johnson, p. 107.

140 Nehemia Gordon and Keith Johnson, p. 31. Unfortunately the film shows contempt for the Jews as the film implies that the Jews alone killed Yeshua, exactly what helped feed the anti-Semitism of the past. Steve Maltz, The People of Many Names, 2005, UK, pp. 143-145.

the name. With her own lips she told us of the dread the name sounded in Jewish ears and what she said accords well with what others have testified. It was in the name Jesus that they were beaten, forced to be baptised, wear badges, were stoned and tortured. Is this the way we are to make the Jews jealous for the gospel? Maltz reminds us that for the Jews it was about life or death (as opposed to the church holding to theological opinions) and that the church has yet to show יֵשׁוּעַ Yeshua to God's own people. It would be remiss if the church did not provide an active reminder of the sorry history of 'Christian' anti-Semitism and make a sincere effort to wipe the slate clean and truly work towards the mysterious entity of the One New Man.'[141] Fruchtenbaum, also a Jewish academic, says that because in Jewish history, most persecutions against the Jews were instigated and carried out by those who called themselves 'Christians' we should refrain from using the name 'Jesus,'[142] with which Stern concurs.[143] Michael Brown, an expert in Jewish Christian apologetics, writer of more than ten books, and a contributor to the Oxford Dictionary of Jewish Religion, says that Jews who believe in יֵשׁוּעַ Yeshua call themselves Messianic Jews, or Hebrew Christians.

> We often use such terms such as Messiah instead of Christ, or Yeshua instead of Jesus because for many Jews, Jesus Christ represents a non-Jewish religious figure, namely, the founder of the Catholic Church and the inspiration of the Crusades. It is because we

---

141 Steve Maltz, Hebraic Church, p. 120.

142 Arnold G. Fruchtenbaum, Israelology: The Missing Link In Systematic Theology, 2001, USA, p. 754.

143 Stern, Jewish New Testament Commentary, p. 262.

> want to think about the real Jesus – the one who came in fulfilment of the Hebrew prophets, the Jewish Redeemer, and the founder of the Messianic faith for all peoples – that we call him Yeshua the Messiah. It is done for the sake of clarity, not duplicity.[144]

In the Disciples prayer[145] Gordon and Johnson write that we say in poetic English, "hallowed be your name." The meaning literally is "May your name be sanctified." The Hebrew manuscript says exactly the same thing. "In both Hebrew and Greek, this is not just a statement of fact but a *call to action* similar to God saying, 'let there be light' during creation...This call to action was a *commandment* that summoned light into existence." "May your name be sanctified" is a call to action, a **commandment to sanctify His name** – in action and deed.[146] As this was taught by **יֵשׁוּעַ** Yeshua, He is referring to **יְהֹוָה** Yehovah, and as **יֵשׁוּעַ** Yeshua is also God then I would say it is very very important to **sanctify His Holy name** as we know it, **יֵשׁוּעַ** Yeshua. Gordon and Johnson remind us of Jeremiah 23:27 which says that the false prophets "hope to cause my people to forget my name." They remark,

> We can choose to be like the false prophets of old and cause our heavenly Father's name to be forgotten, or we can choose the blessing of sanctifying his holy name by proclaiming it to the world.[147]

---

144 Michael Brown, Answering Jewish Objections to Jesus, Vol. One, 2000, USA, pp. 11-12.

145 Also called The Lord's Prayer

146 Nehemia Gordon and Keith Johnson, pp. 97-98.

147 Ibid., p. 108

In Hebrew, every name has a meaning. Names often reflect the person's character or life. It can "denote the essence of the one whom it is given. The name might signify a character role or reveal a certain destiny that person was intended to fulfil." "To know a persons name is to have a relationship with that person. God-fearing Yisra'elites were 'called by the name of the Lord' and hence had a special relationship of accountability to him (Deut. 28:10; see 2 Chron. 7:14)."[148] When studying the תּוֹרָה Torah in the original language you get the benefit of seeing the meaning of names. If you only see the transliterated form of the name you will miss these meanings and connections to the story of each individual. That's why I recommend the reader to learn Hebrew. When I was in Hong Kong preparing to go into China, we were strongly encouraged to quickly begin learning Chinese. I met a lady who was in her 80's studying very hard. That gave me great incentive to learn Chinese as I was only 35. Now that I've been going to 'Jewish' conferences, I have met ladies in their 70's learning Hebrew. I was about 56 when I started learning Hebrew. It's never too late! It would also be helpful too if English commentaries or Study Bibles would assist the reader with these Hebrew names and their meaning.[149] Then the reader can himself see how names reflect the person's life or calling.

Even names of places can be interesting. My favourite is בֵּית לֶחֶם Beit Lechem (Bethlehem, where יֵשׁוּעַ Yeshua was born) meaning 'house of bread.' How fitting is that.

148 Marvin R. Wilson, Exploring Our Hebraic Heritage, 2014, USA, pp. 120-121.

149 David Stern's Complete Jewish Study Bible helps a lot, I just wish it did it more.

יֵשׁוּעַ Yeshua is also the bread of life! Here's another good one. The extended meaning of Bethel and Jacob. Jacob (Gen 28:10-22) had a dream seeing angels ascending and descending upon בֵּית אֵל Bethel (House of God). In the mind of the ancients there were stairs leading to a temple at the top of this ziggurat-like structure. Then in John 1:51, יֵשׁוּעַ Yeshua says that 'you will see heaven opened and the angels of God going up and coming down on the Son of Man.' In Genesis בֵּית אֵל Bethel was at the foot of 'Jacob's ladder;' and in John 1:51 בֵּית אֵל Bethel becomes the person of יֵשׁוּעַ Yeshua. The meaning is that יֵשׁוּעַ Yeshua is saying to נְתַנְאֵל Nathanael (God gives) that he too would see angels going up and coming down, not on בֵּית אֵל Bethel, but on יֵשׁוּעַ Yeshua Himself. This is stated in anticipation of 4:21 where יֵשׁוּעַ Yeshua says, "...the time is coming when you will worship the Father neither on this mountain nor in Yerushalayim."[150]

Gordon and Johnson write,

> Many biblical names refer to God in his role as our heavenly Father, and most of these names begin with the Hebrew word Avi אֲבִי meaning 'my Father.' The simplest of these names is Avi-el אֲבִיאֵל [151](Abiel), meaning 'God is my Father.'[152] Other names express the different ways that God acts as our Heavenly Father, such as Avi-da אֲבִידָע (Abida) 'my Father knows,' Avi-dan אֲבִידָן (Avidan) 'my Father judges,' Avi-ezer אֲבִיעֶזֶר (Abiezer) 'my Father helps,' and Avi-nadav

150 Eli Lizorkin-Eyzenberg, The Jewish Gospel of John, p. 21.
151 I inserted the Hebrew script of the names.
152 1 Sam 9:1.

אֲבִינָדָב (Abinadab) 'my Father gives freely.'[153] There are also names that praise God in his role as our heavenly Father, such as Avi-hud אֲבִיהוּד (Abihud) 'my Father is glorious,' Avi-ram אֲבִירָם (Aviram) 'my Father is exalted,' Avi-tuv אֲבִיטוּב (Abitub) 'my Father is good,' Avi-shalom אֲבִישָׁלוֹם (Abishalom) 'my Father is peace,' and Avi-gayil אֲבִיגָיִל (Abigail) 'my Father is joy.'[154]

A name of interest is Avi-shua[155] אֲבִישׁוּעַ (Abishua), great-grandson of Aron, first High Priest and brother of Moses. It means 'my Father [provides] salvation,' or 'my Father saves.' This name is very similar to Eli-shua[156] אֱלִישׁוּעַ which means 'my God saves.' Taking the two names together they express the deep religious devotion of the Yisraelites that 'my God, my Father provides salvation.' So when יֵשׁוּעַ was teaching the people to pray 'our Father in heaven,' He was conveying all these תּוֹרָה Torah connections "embedded in the hearts and minds, and even the names, of the Jews that came to hear him teach."[157]

There are also Hebrew names that express dedication to the Holy Name. There are over 200 names in the Hebrew Bible that contain יְהֹוָה Yehovah. They often begin with יְהוֹ 'Yeho,' a truncated form of Yehovah, then following that is the word that would describe God's attributes. So 'Yehoshafat' יְהוֹשָׁפָת can be seen as Yeho-shafat; Yeho (Yehovah) shafat (judges), 'Yehovah judges,' Yehoram

153 Gen 25:4; Nu 1:11; Joshua 17:2; 1 Sam 7:1.
154 1Chron 8:3; Nu 16:1; 1Chron 8:11; 1 Ki 15:2; 1 Sam 25:3.
155 Ezra 7:5.
156 2 Sam 5:15.
157 Nehemia Gordon and Keith Johnson, pp. 91-92.

יְהוֹרָם 'Yehovah is exalted,' Jonathan (1 Sam 13-14 etc.) comes from Yehonatan יְהוֹנָתָן 'Yehovah gives,' Yehoyada[158] יְהוֹיָדָע 'Yehovah knows.' Moses changed the name of his servant Hosea יְהוֹשֻׁעַ (He saves) to Joshua 'Yehovah saves.' יֵשׁוּעַ Yeshua is the abbreviated form of Yehoshua יְהוֹשֻׁעַ (Joshua), Yoseph is abbreviated from Yehoseph יְהוֹסֵף 'may Yehovah add,' and John derives from Yehohanan יְהוֹחָנָן 'Yehovah favours.'[159] Peter said, "Whoever calls on the name of יְהוָה Yehovah will be saved." Peter was quoting Joel 3:5.[160] From now on we need to get our names correct. It does not say Jesus – it says יְהוָה Yehovah and Acts 3:6 and 4:11-12 uses the name יֵשׁוּעַ Yeshua. Matthew 1:23 says, "The virgin will conceive and bear a son, and they will call him עִמָּנוּ אֵל 'Immanu El."[161] The way translators have used 'Jesus' they could just as well used names like Bob or George (if they didn't have a meaning anyway.) Of course that wouldn't make sense because עִמָּנוּ Immanu means 'with us' and אֵל El is a word for God – meaning 'God with us.' By the way, when the Jewish crowds (John 12:13) are welcoming יֵשׁוּעַ shouting הוֹשַׁע נָא "Hosanna! (Hoshanna)" did you know that the crowd are crying out, "Save, please!"[162]

Avram אַבְרָם (Abram, Genesis 12) means 'exalted father' and his name is changed (17:5) to אַבְרָהָם Avraham, 'father of a multitude.' In Genesis 12:5 we have Avraham's wife

---

158 2 Ki 3:12; 2 Ki 1:17; 2 Chron 17:8; 2 Sam 8:18 – also Strongs entry 3129 comes from 3083.

159 Nu 13:16; Gen 37:31; Matt 10:2. Nehemia Gordon and Keith Johnson, pp. 107-108.

160 2:32 in non-Jewish Bibles.

161 Isaiah 7:14.

162 See also Eli Lizorkin-Eyzenberg, The Jewish Gospel of John, p. 188.

שָׂרַי Sarai meaning ‘mockery.’ But she gets a new name in chapter 17:15, to **שָׂרָה** Sarah meaning ‘princess, queen.’[163] Elijah (an outstanding Prophet, 2 Ki 2:1) **אֵלִיָּהוּ** Eliyahu means God of **יְהוָה** Yehovah. **אֱלִישָׁע** Elisha is a contraction of **אֱלִישׁוּעַ** Elishua, God of supplication or riches. Now when you follow their lives in the Bible see how it affects your feeling on the story. This is well illustrated by Hagar who in Genesis 16 names a well, reflecting her current life experience. Hagar, being mistreated by Sarai, runs away into the wilderness. But an angel comforts her with a promise that her son would also become a great nation (the promise is still being fulfilled today within Islamic peoples). She responds in vs 13-14, **וַתִּקְרָא שֵׁם־יְהוָה הַדֹּבֵר אֵלֶיהָ אַתָּה אֵל רָאִי כִּי אָמְרָה הֲגַם הֲלֹם רָאִיתִי אַחֲרֵי רֹאִי׃עַל־כֵּן קָרָא לַבְּאֵר בְּאֵר לַחַי רֹאִי** "‘You are EI-roi,’ by which she meant, ‘Have I not gone on seeing after He saw me! Therefore the well was called Beer-lahai-roi, which means ‘well of the Living One who sees me.’[164] The naming of the place was for remembering the event and its significance. ‘El-roi,’ means ‘God who sees me (or ‘God of seeing’)[165] that is ‘the God who looks out for me.’ The "God who hears and sees. This spot would afterwards become holy, a place where God could be found providing for and hearing the cries of His people."[166] God names her son **יִשְׁמָעֵאל** Yishma‘el ‘God pays attention.’[167] The name **נוֹחַ** (Noach) means rest or comfort. After the flood the dove searched for a resting place **מָנוֹחַ** (Manoach) and found it in Noah’s hand. This was the sign that the flood had ended.

---

163 Stern, Complete Jewish Study Bible.
164 Edited by Rabbi Tuly Weisz, The Israel Bible, p. 38.
165 Stern, Complete Jewish Study Bible.
166 John F. Walvoord and Roy B. Zuck, The Bible Knowledge Commentary, Old Testament, 1985, USA, p. 57.
167 Stern, Complete Jewish Study Bible.

Another good example is in John 11 where אֶלְעָזָר Lazarus is raised from death. How prophetic, as his name means, 'God will help.'[168] Thinking of John the Baptist, יוֹחָנָן Yochanan means 'God's grace.' This time when you read "there was a man sent from God whose name was יוֹחָנָן Yochanan," does that not give colour to the revelation? He was the "voice of one calling in the wilderness, preparing the way of the Lord." During his ministry, John was the only real representative of God's light and came to testify to that light of God Himself, יֵשׁוּעַ Yeshua, the Son of God.[169]

The more the Hebrew Bible is read from a Jewish world-view, the more the importance of names is brought home to the reader. Lizorkin-Eyzenberg, president of Israel Bible Center, in his new book, also raised the issue of names and said that

> Regardless of our personal opinions and practices, we should value the search for much-need authenticity and originality in faithful living. In one way or another, we should affirm the Israelite roots and character of our modern prayers...[170]

As a bare minimum, especially when saying the names of God and יֵשׁוּעַ it is incumbent that in affirming our Jewish heritage we use authentic real Hebrew names!

---

168 Eli Lizorkin-Eyzenberg, The Jewish Gospel of John, p. 170.
169 Eli Lizorkin-Eyzenberg, The Jewish Gospel of John, pp. 4-5.
170 Eli Lizorkin-Eyzenberg, Jewish Insights Into Scripture, Israel Bible Center, p. 89.

The Name Parable

Scott Nelson wrote a very good article[171] concerning יֵשׁוּעַ Yeshua's name which is most appropriate and worthy of summary. There once was a missionary, Barbara (Barb) Mayhew, who worked in the Philippines. After a number of years, she moved back home to the USA, but ten years later she was urged to return to the Philippines because the people there were still thinking so highly of her, even dedicating a church to her. Some Filipinos wanted to see her so badly they were considering going to the USA to find her. Barb didn't want them to do that so she decided to go to them, but had to wait three weeks to fulfil home commitments. Finally, Barb arrived to her past mission field, but for some reason all the villagers knew her now as Zyka Zeejerst. That name sounded to Barb very harsh, but they really believed it was her name and said it with excited love. She also found out that others also used it as a curse word.

It turns out that one Filipino, Tawani, did go to the USA in search of Zyka Zeejerst, just as Barb was on her way to the Philippines. So they just missed each other. Tawani arrives in Barb's home town and asks a store clerk for Zyka Zeejerst. But to her horror he does not know Zyka Zeejerst, a famous missionary! As she approached others, neither did they know Zyka Zeejerst. In desperation she finally pulls out an old photo and now people recognize her and said her name was Barbara Mayhew. Barb was in the Philippines for two months now and began missing her real name – Zyka Zeejerst sounding too harsh. Though she wanted to tell the

171 Scott Nelson, THE NAME – A Modern Parable, http//www.judaismvschristianity.com/parable.htm The parable is very creative and worth reading.

villagers her real name, she realized they were in love with the name Zyka Zeejerst as much as with her.

Then some time later, Tawani arrives back in the Philippines. All the villagers excitedly inform her that Zyka Zeejerst was with them. Barb recognizes Tawani and says, "Hello Tawani." Tawani responds, "Barb? Barb Mayhew?" The villagers are in shock, but Barb says, "Yes my name is Barb. Thank you thank you Tawani...you know who I am." Nelson writes (and I quote him at length):

> Though this story is fiction, it was written as a parable to illustrate a problem that exists among the English speaking people concerning a real person and his name. That person is the one known as *Jesus Christ.*
>
> Did you know that if you could go back to the time of the twelve apostles, if you walked up to Peter and said, 'Please take me to see *Jesus Christ*', Peter would get a puzzled look on his face and say the equivalent of, 'Who, or what is that?' Did you know that no one who followed *Jesus* was capable of pronouncing in English the name 'Jesus' even if they tried? The truth is, if you *could* go back in time and meet Peter, he would probably say something like, 'Come, and I will show you Y'shua the Messiah.' The sad truth of the matter is that the harsh sounding name of *Jesus Christ* is the equivalent of Zyka Zeejerst as far as the Messiah, the Son of God is concerned. You might be inclined to think the comparison isn't fair and the name Zyka Zeejerst sounds far more harsh than the name

Jesus Christ. If so, this is a subliminal bias due to the fact that you have come to love the name *Jesus Christ*. Look closely at the name Zyka Zeejerst. It is a simple rearrangement of every sound in the name *Jesus Christ*. [And is it any wonder why the name is used frequently as a curse word?]

What will you do? There is no doubt that many prayers that have been prayed in the name of 'Jesus' have been answered. I can personally attest to this fact. But this does not prove that *Jesus* is the Messiah's true name. What it does indicate is that God is good and merciful in spite of our ignorance. It proves that God judges the heart of man and not his head. He is a righteous judge and judges a man on what his heart causes him to do with what he *does* know. He does not judge a man simply on the basis of what he does *not* know. If God were to wait until a man's understanding were perfect, man would never receive anything from Him. We should be eternally grateful to God for His goodness toward us even while we are ignorant of so much truth. But you are now no longer ignorant of the truth concerning the name of His Son, Yeshua the Messiah.

The good news is that in this day of information, it is not necessary for anyone to live in ignorance any longer. And unlike Greek and Latin, the English language contains all the sounds necessary to accurately pronounce the Hebrew name *Y'shua*. You may continue calling *Yeshua* the equivalent of *Zyka Zeejerst* if you chose. You may even support your choice with a cliché like 'A rose by any other name is still a rose', but you will have missed the whole point of the parable. We are not dealing with inanimate vegetation. We are talking about a living being who feels many things just as you or I would. And this person obviously considers a name as well as an accurate knowledge of him of great importance. Consider how he might feel about being called "*Jesus*" while knowing that you know better. How would you feel? Unloved? Do you truly love him enough to care? Can you imagine how Barb felt when she finally heard her true name spoken by someone who cared so much for her? And consider this: If you are a person who teaches others, on what grounds can you legitimately expect others to change their ways when you present them with an irrefutable argument if you yourself are not willing to do the same?

It's not as hard to change as you might think. As you begin to pray in 'Yeshua's' name and refer to him as 'Yeshua' in your discussions, as well as say 'Yeshua' when you see the name *Jesus* in print, over time, you will wonder how you ever got along without his true name. You will find that 'Jesus' is no longer 'the sweetest name I know.' The name *Yeshua* will have become far sweeter! I can personally attest to this as well.

You can also be a significant part of this non-denominational effort to bring back our Lord's true name. You can print out this article and read it at your next family devotional time, your next Bible study, prayer breakfast, Sunday-school class, or any other appropriate gathering of those who claim to love *"Jesus"*. Then make a commitment with them to use only the Lord's true name *Yeshua*, and the title, *the Messiah* instead of the harsh sounding Greek word *Christ*. If others ask why you use the name *Yeshua* instead of *Jesus*, you can give them a copy of this article. You can also help to be a part of the movement to return Yeshua's name by copying, pasting, and forwarding this article to as many of your friends and family who love the Lord as you can. Hopefully, in time, even Bible publishers may feel the need to print new *Yeshua-correct* Bibles.

Consider this possibility. It could very well be that it is God's intention to return the true name of His Son *Yeshua* to those who truly love him at this time soon before Yeshua's return.

So what *will* you do with the new knowledge you now possess? What you do with it will speak volumes in heaven. Listen to the importance that God the Father places on knowing a name.

'Because he has set his love upon Me, therefore I will deliver him; I will set him on high, **because he has known My name**. He shall call upon Me, and I will answer him; I will be with him in trouble; I will deliver him and honor him. With long life will I satisfy him, and show him My salvation.' Psalm 91:14-16.

If someone were to prove conclusively that the name 'Jesus' was chosen not because of a conspiracy as I have proposed above or not because of overt hostility to Judaism – I am inclined to think that even this could be irrelevant. As noted above and in part two of this volume, there are plenty of other reasons we need to use יֵשׁוּעַ Yeshua's name. The bottom line is that names are important, we certainly now know יֵשׁוּעַ Yeshua's real name, we can pronounce it, and scripture demands the use of Gods proper name! Do you love יֵשׁוּעַ Yeshua enough to call Him יֵשׁוּעַ Yeshua?

I know of some people who would like to use the name יֵשׁוּעַ Yeshua but do not solely because of habit. May I suggest that these people, as I have done with other words (see part two), wake up one morning and commit to God and to themselves to consciously refuse to use the word 'Jesus.' To force themselves to get into the habit of using God's name יֵשׁוּעַ Yeshua.

"If we had forgotten the name of God or spread out our hands to a foreign god, wouldn't God have discovered this, since he knows the secrets of the heart?" (Psalm 44:20-21). Is this not a good incentive to re-assess the name 'Jesus'? Most people, if they have used the name 'Jesus' in the past, probably did so in good faith. It is the name we were brought up with. The whole church uses the name. Nehemia Gordon gently reminds us though that it is important to try to get things right when we can. Now with better information surely we should act on that better information. We need always to return to truth when we find it and do the best we can with what we learn.[172] One time when speaking to a friend of mine, every time he said the name

172 Nehemia Gordon, YouTube, The Origins of Yaweh, November 7, 2018.

Jesus I called him Bob (his name was not Bob). After a while he was getting annoyed with me calling him Bob. So I said, well could it be יֵשׁוּעַ Yeshua feels the same way now that you know His real name? If the name 'Jesus' was the product of anti-Semitism I strongly propose we get used to saying His real name. Furthermore יֵשׁוּעַ Yeshua is God, a name of utmost reverence. And because the name 'Jesus' is appalling to the ears of many Jews, whom we are to provoke to jealousy, we are in an age where its time to repent and change our ways and our language. This is what part two of this monograph is about.

Part Two

Provoking יִשְׂרָאֵל Yisra'el to jealousy

Stern refers us here to Romans 11:11-15. שָׁאוּל Sha'ul (Paul) gives the Christians in Rome their mission 'to provoke יִשְׂרָאֵל Yisra'el to jealousy' for יֵשׁוּעַ Yeshua their Messiah.

> שָׁאוּל Sha'ul, the emissary to the Gentiles (v. 13), had just written that he would give up even his own salvation to see his people saved (9:3-4). Thus, as their emissary, the Gentile believer has something of the same calling. The outcome would be 'life from the dead' (Rom. 11:15).
>
> Whereas chronologically the good news was preached first to the Jew and thereafter to all nations (Acts 1:8; Rom.1:16;), the question must be asked: How can a Gentile believer present an effective witness to the Jewish people of their own Messiah if the delivery of the message is non-Jewish and culturally stripped of its Jewish origins? Jews will never be provoked to jealousy by a non-Jewish message and it would be seen as counterfeit. For all of Yisra'el to declare, בָּרוּךְ הַבָּא בְּשֵׁם יְהֹוָה[173] 'Blessed is he who comes in the name of Yehovah,' the message must be authentically Jewish.
>
> Humility as a 'wild olive [branch]' (Rom.11:17), will be more effective in provoking the Jewish people to jealousy. The Gentile believer must not

173 Matthew 23:39 which is from Psalms 118:26. I inserted all Hebrew script.

> be arrogant towards the Jews – that is, condescending toward God's chosen people (v.18). The non-Jew needs to remember that salvation came to us in part because of Yisra'el's stubbornness ('some of the branches were broken off'), so they shouldn't boast against the 'natural branches.' Salvation is a free gift from God and the partial hardening of Jewish hearts toward Yeshua means salvation for them (vv.22-24).[174]

Sterns continues to state that apart from Christian persecution of Jews, another reason the Jewish people do not accept יֵשׁוּעַ as the Messiah is that it

> arises partly from the way Christianity presents itself, but also from the alienation induced by most New Testament translations. With their Gentile Christian cultural trappings and their anti-Jewish theological underpinnings, they lead many Jews to see the New Testament as a Gentile book about a Gentile god. The Jesus portrayed therein seems to bear little relationship to Jewish life. It becomes hard for a Jew to experience Yeshua the Messiah as who he really is, namely, as a friend to every Jewish heart.[175]

Ilse Posselt in his article 'Restoring the Truth after Replacement Theology,' says,

---

174 Stern, The Complete Jewish Study Bible, p. 1623.

175 Ibid., p. xlvi. And that is why Stern produced The Complete Jewish Study Bible, as it helps to eliminate some of the linguistic, cultural, and theological obstacles.

> Recognizing the teaching [replacement theology] as false is certainly a watershed event in church history. However, if we as a body of believers are to move forward, its denouncement should surely be but the first step in the restoring the truth.

It is good to admit that we ignored Romans 11 which taught that

> we were supposed to derive our sustenance to grow and develop from the roots burrowed in biblical covenant through the cultivated olive tree or 'the root supports you' as Romans 11:18 instructs. Yet history teaches that we chose instead to draw our nourishment from the root of replacement theology and thus fed and matured on its destructive falsehoods.
>
> Psychology says that we are all, to some extent, the products of our past; our current identity shaped by the views, opinions and beliefs we held as true. The body of believers is no exception. And supersessionism became part of the church's past nearly 1,900 years ago, thus shaping its identity through the views, opinions and beliefs it held as truth for nearly two millennia.
>
> The result of generations of twisted teachings is, unfortunately, a church where supersessionism has become interwoven – sometimes undetectably – into fundamental aspects of our identity...Apart from distorting our view towards the Jewish people,

Soulen[176] explains, it also birthed, influenced and molded much of our classic Christian narrative and the church's core beliefs and praxis.

As such, a mere acknowledgement of its prevalence in our past and a rejection of the teaching going forward will do little to erase its legacy and inheritance. In fact, denouncing supersessionism, Soulen holds, is rather pointless unless we as a church are willing to take the next step and reassess the theological, ecclesiastical and evangelistic principles that form the foundation of Christianity.

A mammoth undertaking, no doubt. Yet perhaps the starting point of such a journey should be exploring the identity of the one whom our very existence as a church rests.[177]

One of the most effective ways in which the church today can counteract the effects of nearly 2000 years of replacement theology is by gaining a thorough understanding of the principles of the Jewish faith, says Prof. Brad Young.[178] … We have to be willing to peel back the layers of tradition to reveal [Yeshua] the Jew...

Yet although the church appears ready to acknowledge his ethnicity, he says, we often seem less inclined to consider and embrace the

176 Dr Kendall Soulen is a leading author and Prof. of Systematic Theology.

177 Ilse Posselt, The Jerusalem Post, Oct 2016, p. 27.

178 Professor of Biblical Literature in Judeo-Christian Studies and author of many books.

implications of his heritage on our theology. As a result, the church, to a large extent, hails [Yeshua] as a Jew by birth, but continues to interpret his theology as Christian.

Yet over time, the Hebraic blueprint familiar to [Yeshua], his followers and the early church made way for the Hellenistic or Greek worldview, which continues to dominate much of Western society today. With these two mindsets literally worlds apart in pattern of thought, values, interpretation and perceptions, we run the risk of attempting to understand [Yeshua] and interpret the Scriptures through the lens of Greek thinking.

Consequently, much is often lost in the translation from one worldview to another. And unless we as the church are willing to set aside our Hellenistic outlook in favor of the context of the original Hebrew culture and setting, Young cautions, we are in danger of misinterpreting many of [Yeshua] sayings and misunderstanding parts of his message. In fact, by failing to recognize the impact of the Jewishness of [Yeshua] and its enduring influence on believers today, he warns, we will miss much of His essence altogether.

In short, we have to swap our Hellenistic lenses for Hebrew ones."[179]

---

179 Brad Young as cited by Ilse Posselt, The Jerusalem Post, Oct 2016, pp. 28-29.

To begin this process I suggest we start purchasing commentaries and books written by Rabbis and Jewish scholars. For instance, and I highly recommend it, 'The Complete Jewish Study Bible,' the text was translated by David Stern[180] as it has not only a useful commentary but all names are in Hebrew (often with their meaning) and you will get used to saying **יֵשׁוּעַ** Yeshua. Likewise, 'The Israel Bible,'[181] is very good.

As we have studied, names in Hebrew have meaning and as we learn more, we should accommodate what we learn. For a start could we not clean up our vocabulary? Below I suggest a few concepts, names or labels that we could do well to abandon. I begin with using the ridiculous name 'Jehovah'.

'Jehovah'

Hebrew does not have the sound 'J'! Most modern translations no longer use this name, seeing it as a mistake. Bivin adds, Furthermore 'Jehovah' has no meaning. The non-word 'Jehovah' illustrates "so vividly Christians' continuing lack of understanding of Hebrew language and Jewish practice."[182]

---

180 (2016, Hendrickson Publishers). D. Stern earned a Ph.D. and was a professor before he met **יֵשׁוּעַ**, then got a Master of Divinity degree and did graduate work at the University of Judaism. He then moved to Israel in 1979. He wrote a commentary for the R.C. and the 'Messianic Jewish Manifesto. These last two books are a must for those with not yet a Jewish commentary.

181 Edited by Rabbi Tuly Weisz, The Israel Bible.

182 David Bivin, New Light on the Words of Jesus, pp. 56-57.

'Yaweh' or 'Yahweh'

Where did the name 'Yaweh' come from? From the Hebrew grammarian Wilhelm Gesenius. All biblical Hebrew Lexicons are based on the works of the German rationalist Gesenius (Maltz comments, "not a good start, with something of such importance to the faith community…"). In his 1833 Hebrew grammar dictionary he states that the name 'Yaweh' was suggested by church father Theadoris Syrus. For about 200 years there was a debate over the name יְהוָה – was it 'Yaweh' or Yehovah'? In the end Gesenius decided for 'Yaweh'. Academia worldwide quickly followed his advice. But later Gesenius made an important discovery and admits this in his 1857 dictionary. He says it was a huge mistake to chose in favour of 'Yaweh'. It appears that there was an Egyptian deity that both the Hebrew and Latin's worshipped and the deity's name sounded very similar to 'Yaweh.' Gesenius himself never even got the sound first hand but even possibly third hand. But it was too late for the academia, they were now entrenched with the old word and were not interested in switching for the proper name, 'Yehovah.'[183] Even the *Anchor Bible Dictionary* 1992 admitted that Yaweh was nothing more than 'a scholarly guess.'[184] Maltz says "…this cannot be correct, just from the simplest facts of Hebrew grammar, the pronunciation of the letters." A better choice would have at least been Yahveh.[185]

183 Nehemia Gordon, the story as related on YouTube, I found difficult to write out. I recommend the reader see it for themselves, The Origins of Yaweh, Nov. 7, 2018.

184 Nehemia Gordon and Keith Johnson, p. 99.

185 Steve Maltz, God's Signature, 2012, UK., p. 75

Gordon continues: Yaweh cannot fit in with the explanation of God's name in Exodus 3:14-15. The explanation is seen as:

הָיָה	הֹוֶה	יִהְיֶה
he who was	he who is	he who will be, or he who is to come

Yaweh can not even mean – he who was, he who is, he who is to come. But the name יְהֹוָה Yehovah does![186]

יְהֹוָה 'Yehovah'

In Exodus 3:15 we read,

> אֱלֹהִים God said further to מֹשֶׁה Moshe (Moses), "Say this to the people of Israel: יְהֹוָה Yehovah, the God of your fathers, the God of אַבְרָהָם Avraham, the God of יִצְחָק Yitz'chak (Isaac) and the God of יַעֲקֹב Ya'akov (Jacob), has sent me to you." This is my name forever; this is how I am to be remembered generation to generation.[187]

Nehemia Gordon commenting on Exodus 3:15 says,

> 'This is my name forever, this is זִכְרִי *zikhri*, my **mention**, from generation to generation.' This means we are required by scripture to *mention* Him by his eternal name יְהֹוָה Yehovah! This fits with the explicit commandment to swear by the name

---

186 YouTube, The Origins of Yaweh, Nov. 7, 2018.

187 See also Nehemiah Gordon, The Hebrew Yeshua vs. the Greek Jesus, pp. 63-64.

יְהוָה Yehovah. For example, Deuteronomy 6:13[188] 'You shall fear יְהוָה Yehovah your God, and you shall worship Him, and **in His name shall you swear** [**וּבִשְׁמוֹ תִּשָּׁבֵעַ**].' This is a clear and explicit commandment to make oaths in the name of יְהוָה Yehovah. Similarly, Deuteronomy 10:20, 'יְהוָה Yehovah your God you shall fear, and Him shall you worship, and to him shall you cling, and in His name shall you swear.'

There is actually a very important end-times prophesy in Jeremiah 12:16 related to the vow formula, 'As YHWH lives': And it shall be if they nevertheless learn the way of My people to swear in my name 'As YHWH lives' [**לְהִשָּׁבֵעַ בִּשְׁמִי חַי־יְהוָה**] in the way that they taught My people to swear by Ba'al, then they will be built up among my people. (Jeremiah 12:16)

I was always fascinated with this prophecy because it is speaking to the Gentiles, not the Israelites! It is directed at those Gentiles who taught Israel to swear by Baal. If these Gentiles will learn to swear 'As YHWH lives' then they will become a part of the covenant-nation. Obviously this has not happened yet… But this is a promise that in the end-time the Gentiles will learn to swear in the name of YHWH and through this they will be built into Israel.[189]

188 and 10:20

189 Nehemiah Gordon, p. 64.

Clearly יְהֹוָה Yehovah's name is intended to be pronounced even by Gentiles! (See also Psalm 148:11-13). It is now obvious why we all need to know God's name. The ancient Rabbis instituted a ban[190] on pronouncing יְהֹוָה so as a result substitutes were used, אֲדוֹנָי Adonai being the most common. Gordon, being a Karaite,[191] and therefore not under the ban, would have no problem with this prohibition. Based on his research he's found many proofs that יְהֹוָה is indeed pronounced as 'Yehovah.' For example, in the oldest vocalized manuscripts we have יְהֹוָה Yehovah many times.[192] For the defence of the name יְהֹוָה Yehovah, see the various YouTube programs of Nehemia Gordon. One way to sanctify יְהֹוָה Yehovah's name is to proclaim His name to the whole world, "so that all the peoples of the earth will know your name and fear you" (1 Kings 8:43). This is His name forever and for all generations (Exodus 3:15). It is very interesting that Rabbi Tuly Weisz, in The Israel Bible, has יְהֹוָה Yehovah vocalized in the Hebrew script – the same as that which Gordon has advocated!

The Rabbinic ban on using יְהֹוָה Yehovah was never intended to be permanent according to the Rabbis. His name will once again be spoken aloud when the Messiah reigns as king on this earth. Zechariah 14:9 reads, "Then יְהֹוָה Yehovah will be king over the whole world. On that day יְהֹוָה Yehovah will be the only one, and his name will be the only name."[193] The Rabbis understand this to say that

190 Nehemia Gordon and Keith Johnson, p. 99.

191 One whose exclusive loyalty is the Hebrew Scriptures and not to the Oral Torah; Gordon, The Hebrew Yeshua vs. the Greek Jesus, pp. 24-26.

192 Nehemia Gordon and Keith Johnson, p. 100.

193 Nehemia Gordon and Keith Johnson, p. 101.

in the end-times all mankind would once again call upon the actual name of יְהֹוָה Yehovah. Despite this ban on The Name, it still appeared *written out* in the תּוֹרָה Torah 6,828 times. In obedience to the ban on The Name, the Rabbis taught the translators of the KJB to use the word 'LORD' (which is why most English Bibles do the same). But the KJB still employed the name 'Yehovah' seven times because they believed that replacing The Name in certain places would not make any sense. For example, Psalm 83:19 says, "Let them know that you alone, whose name is יְהֹוָה, are the Most High over all the earth." The KJB correctly used 'Yehovah'; The New International Version, English Standard Version, and probably most versions very sadly and most incorrectly threw in the name 'LORD.' I totally agree with Gordon when he says that when the translators substituted יְהֹוָה for 'LORD' they have completely changed the meaning of the verse; the name of God is no longer יְהֹוָה Yehovah but rather 'the LORD.'[194] But as said before, Deuteronomy 6:13 (and 10:20) says, וּבִשְׁמוֹ תִּשָּׁבֵעַ and by His name swear – meaning we are required by scripture to speak out His eternal name יְהֹוָה Yehovah. Before the Rabbinic ban on The Name, we see that in the Book of Rut (Ruth),[195] the name was encouraged. Boaz says יְהֹוָה עִמָּכֶם וַיֹּאמְרוּ לוֹ יְבָרֶכְךָ יְהֹוָה (to the harvesters) יְהֹוָה Yehovah be with you and they answered, יְהֹוָה Yehovah bless you. Boaz gives us all an excellent example of how we can greet one another, in everyday speech, using the name of יְהֹוָה Yehovah.[196]

---

194 Nehemia Gordon and Keith Johnson, pp. 103-105.

195 רוּת 2:4

196 Nehemia Gordon and Keith Johnson, p. 106.

Not only will we be speaking the Lord's name properly in the end times but also we will be speaking more Hebrew. Al Garza informs us,

> A Midrash on the [מִגְדָּל בָּבֶל] Migdal Bavel (Tower of Babel) teaches that at the end of time all people will once again speak one language and that will be a purified form of the Hebrew tongue. There is also d'rash on the verse: 'For then I will make the peoples pure of speech, so that they all invoke [יְהֹוָה Yehovah] by name and serve Him with one accord' (Zeph 3:9) that indicates the same.[197]

Tuly Weisz concurs that the שָׂפָה בְרוּרָה pure language is the Hebrew language.

> In future times, the world will begin to learn Hebrew, the language of creation. This promise has begun to come true in our age. Not only has the Hebrew language been revitalized over the past century as the spoken language in the Jewish homeland, but in more recent years, thousands of non-Jews have also begun to study Hebrew as a way to connect with their creator and gain a deeper understanding of the Bible.[198]

I again suggest that we contemplate learning Hebrew as this provides an antidote to the erroneous division of the Holy Scriptures as currently practised in the Gentile church.

---

197 Al Garza, The Hebrew New Testament, p. 11.
198 Rabbi Tuly Weisz, The Israel Bible, p. 28.

'Old Testament and New Testament'

Walter Kaiser begins,

> The designation 'Old Testament' is in itself anachronistic, for nowhere in the...Bible does the term occur. Actually, it was the Alexandrian church father Origen (c.185-c.254) who gave us this nomenclature, based in part on God's promise in Jeremiah 31:31 of a 'new covenant' – hence his 'New Testament'. But both the label and the translation are misleading; it is only ecclesiastical convention that dictates our continued use of this term for that group of biblical books that the Jews referred to as 'the writings,' 'the Scriptures,' and 'the Law and the Prophets.'[199]

Biblically speaking, Stern adds, 'Old' here merely means 'earlier.'[200]

> But Jeremiah's promise of a 'New Covenant' (Jer 31:31-34) appears to many to mean that the program announced to Abraham and David has been superceded, or at least attenuated. However, this confusion results from attaching a modern meaning to a word 'new'. In Jeremiah's usage it meant only to 'renew,' as can be seen from the use of the same Hebrew word for the 'new moon.' This is also true of most of the contents of the previous

199 Walter C. Kaiser, Jr., Toward Rediscovering The Old Testament, 1987, USA, p. 35.

200 Stern, The Complete Jewish Study Bible, p. xxx.

promises made to Abraham, Isaac, Jacob, and David.[201]

Stern comments that in Greek there are two words for 'new': *kainos* and *'neos.'* N*eos* means 'new' as in something which has never existed before. But *kainos* "carries overtones of freshness and renewal of something which existed." The phrase 'New Covenant' is always *kainos.* Actually in a very real way the New Covenant renews the Old covenant.[202] Wilson concurs saying that 'new' suggests a 'refreshing,' 'renewing,' or 'recent updating' of the original covenant of grace that became enlarged anew and to its fullest expression of grace in the coming of [**יֵשׁוּעַ** Yeshua]."[203]

The first man to popularize such a division was the heretic Marcion. He wrongly believed (about 138 AD) the O.T. God was inferior to the N.T. God; actually an earlier form of replacement theology. His heresy was one of the first for the church to face. He argued that the **תּוֹרָה** Torah had no authoritative revelation and fought to have it removed completely. The R.C. God was one of love. Marcion's goal was to rid Christianity of all traces of Judaism. Though condemned as a heretic, very unfortunate was the retaining of his labels/categorization of the two testaments.[204]

---

201 Walter C. Kaiser, Jr., Toward Rediscovering The Old Testament, pp. 25-26.

202 Stern, Jewish New Testament Commentary, p. 690.

203 Marvin R. Wilson, Exploring Our Hebraic Heritage, p. 71; Rabbi John Fischer, How Jewish is Christianity?, p. 54. Ariel Berkowitz gives the name 'Newer Covenant Scriptures'. Foreword in David Friedman, They Loved The Torah.

204 Jacob Vince, In Touch mag., (Christian Friends of Israel), No 191, 2017, p. 2; Marvin R. Wilson, Our Father Abraham, pp. 108-109;

Rabbi Tuly Weisz, in his introduction to The Israel Bible, adds that while the **תָּנָ״ךְ** Tanakh[205] has "been referred to as the 'Old Testament,' many Jews reject this label since it implies the replacement of the Hebrew Bible with something newer..."[206]

Sharon Sanders comments:

> Labels have power and they affect how people perceive things and the extent to which they value them. For Jews, the Torah is the basis of Judaism, the foundational document that defines their faith as well as their relationship with God and our fellow man. As former British Chief Rabbi Jonathan Sacks once pointed out, 'One of the most tragic moments in Western civilization came when Christians began distinguishing between what they called 'the Old Testament God of vengeance' as opposed to the 'New Testament God of love.' This is not a small error. One trembles to think how many Jews lost their lives because of it...For countless ages God's Voice which spoke to Moses, has been labelled 'Archaic, obsolete, and old-

---

Wilson, Exploring Our Hebraic Heritage, p. 26; Steve Maltz, How The Church Lost The Truth, p. 48 and Shalom, pp. 30-31.

205 Also spelt as Tenach, an acronym made from the first letters of the 3 main divisions of the Hebrew Bible. Torah-5 books of Moses, Nevi'im-prophets, and Chetuvim (or K'tuvim) - writings. See Nehemiah Gordon, The Hebrew Yeshua vs. the Greek Jesus, p. xiii; Stern, The Complete Jewish Study Bible, p. xxviii #2.

206 P. xix.

fashioned,' something like an old car parked in a garage, discarded and forgotten.[207]

...the Jewish scriptures, so commonly categorized wrongly with the label 'Old' Testament [are] mislabelled, impolite and ill-informed characterization of the books of the Bible.

Because we live in Israel, תּוֹרָה Torah or תָּנַךְ Tanach come spontaneously to believers in the land. However, most of the world's Christians...employ and practice using the world "Old" Testament when speaking of the first part of the Bible. It is a misnomer. Labelling the enduring word of God in a wrong or inaccurate way is a serious rebellion against God. This error is a faux pas, or more accurately, a failure of the Christian Church. Here in Israel, we know it is as the Living Word, alive and real. It is sad that we have had a lack of education in this area in order for inherited errors to be corrected. God only knows how many Jewish people died because of Christians believing that 'their books' were finished, obsolete and outdated.[208]

...By labelling God's word as 'Old' (the enduring, eternal, everlasting, immortal, imperishable, ongoing, perpetual, and timeless Scriptures, to describe just a few biblical classifications) is a serious insult to our Jewish friends. Clearly, the

207 Sharon Sanders, For Zion's Sake, Fourth Quarter, 2017, Christian Friends of Israel, p. 6.

208 Sharon Sanders, For Zion's Sake, Fourth Quarter, 2017, p. 4.

> Lord established the Torah, and based His teachings on Torah. Throughout the [R.C.] continually He said, 'It is written.' Since there was no [R.C.] at the time [Yeshua] was teaching, it is crystal clear that [Yeshua] laid it out clearly that He was pointing people where to go for answers.[209]

The Tanach is not archaic, like an old shoe, a relic of a bygone era, or old-fashioned. Nor is it superseded, abrogated, annulled, done away with, or replaced.[210] "It was the Jewish scrolls He unrolled in synagogues" and read.[211] What we have called 'the Law' are actually instruction and teaching. We need a burning desire for both the R.C. and תְּנַךְ Tanach. When יֵשׁוּעַ Yeshua returns, תּוֹרָה Torah will go forth from Zion (Is 2:3; Micah 4:2).[212] In Matthew 5:18, יֵשׁוּעַ Yeshua said not even the smallest letter would be dropped until He returns and anyone who disregards it will be regarded as the smallest in the Kingdom – so beware of the way we treat the Tanach. Even Revelation (22:19) forbids the taking away of scripture. But if we neglect it and never look at it, is that not tantamount to deleting the Words of God? תּוֹרָה Torah is the thoughts of Gods heart (Jeremiah 23:20). Sanders informs us that even the *Jerusalem Post* in a headline article said, 'Stop calling it the Old Testament!' [213] Rich Bank likewise wrote, "Avoid referring to the Holy (Hebrew) Bible as the 'Old Testament...there can be nothing 'old' about the Hebrew Bible."[214] We now can see, the Jews who were scattered,

---

209 Ibid.

210 Marvin Wilson, Exploring Our Hebraic Heritage, p. 26.

211 Sharon Sanders, For Zion's Sake, Fourth Quarter, 2017, p. 4.

212 Ibid., pp. 4-5.

213 For Zion's Sake, Fourth Quarter, 2017, p. 5.

214 Rich Bank, The Everything JUDAISM BOOK, 2002, USA, p. 50.

are now back in their promised land – in fulfilment of the Abrahamic and Mosaic covenants! Especially as we see תּוֹרָה Torah prophesies being fulfilled, we can now renew our faith in all scripture and be as the Bereans searching for truth – shredding our misuse and centuries of misunderstanding of תּוֹרָה Torah. Furthermore, תּוֹרָה Torah has 120 prophesies yet to be fulfilled; we should be aware of them and ought to be praying and working for their fulfilment.

'Law'

What about the term 'Law'? David Friedman begins by saying,

> It would be wrong to define the Torah as *Law* as is done so often by commentators, translators, and teachers. The richness of the Torah is evidenced by its makeup – narrative history, instructions, instructional songs and poems, legal codes, genealogies, ethical instructions, and covenants. The fuller meaning of the term *Torah* refers to the full instruction given by God to the Jewish people….[215]

Brad Young informs us that

> Almost all English translations of the Bible translate the Hebrew word *torah* as "Law." Modern Western Christians often have, as a result, received a distorted perspective of Torah from uninformed preaching and Sunday school teachings. It is indeed

215 David Friedman, They Loved The Torah, preface.

> a legal code with strict requirements, and in its most narrow sense, sometimes Torah can mean law. But 'law' can also be a very misleading translation. To understand Torah strictly as law would be like translating the word *parent* as 'disciplinarian.' Such a translation produces an unfair characterization of what a parent truly is. Describing Torah only as law is similarly lacking.
>
> The verb *yarah*, from which the noun *torah* comes, means 'to shoot at a target with force and accuracy.' It also means 'revelation' and first and foremost refers to a revelation of the nature and character of God, and how to live life to its fullest measure in a way that is pleasing to God. It means to shoot and hit the target accurately based upon the revelation of God...its teachings give greater meaning to every dimension of a person's life.[216]

Dr Moseley adds that

> According to modern scholarship, the English word 'law' is a poor translation of the Greek word *nomos*, which Paul used frequently in the epistles. The meaning and scope of nomos is far greater than the idea behind our English concept of law. Paul was 100% Jewish, and when he spoke of the law, he was

---

216 Brad H. Young, Meet The Rabbis, p. 39; see also Walter C. Kaiser, Jr., Toward Rediscovering The Old Testament, p. 172 and Toward Old Testament Ethics, 1983, USA, p. 21. In Steve Maltz's words, the Torah "is a most misunderstood word by Christians today, who usually translate it as 'law' or, should I say 'LAW', the *unyielding, stifling, restrictive Old Testament concept that we are all thankfully free from now*. This is complete nonsense..." Steve Maltz, How The Church Lost The Way, pp. 141-142 and Shalom, p. 182.

> thinking in terms of Torah, the way of life for the believer.[217]

So we see that the word תּוֹרָה Torah, that we have erroneously translated as 'Law' actually has a very different emphasis in Hebrew. We learn it means 'to point out, teach, instruct, or give direction.' תּוֹרָה Torah, then, is יְהוָה Yehovah's instruction to man that we are to obey; it is God's loving guidance. תּוֹרָה Torah, as we can see, includes the story of Creation, the Fall, the choosing of Avraham, and the Jewish people's deliverance from slavery[218] Fisher says that,

> Theologically, the ancient covenants worked more like documents of grace and love rather than instruments of law. In fact, Deuteronomy 7:12 even calls the Torah a 'covenant of love,' as does Nehemiah 9:32. The graciousness of God spills out from the very first words of the condensed form of the covenant: 'I am the Lord your God, who brought you out of Egypt, out of the land of slavery' (Exodus 20:2). This becomes the 'first' commandment' according to classic Jewish perspective, and rightly so and it is replete with grace.[219]

---

217 Dr. Ron Moseley, Yeshua, 1996, USA, p. 59. For an in-depth study on the negative usage of law see pp. 44-72.

218 Lois Tverberg with Bruce Okkema, Listening to the Language of the Bible, 2006, USA, pp. 9-10; Rob Richards, Has God finished with Israel, 2000, UK, pp. 97-101.

219 Rabbi John Fisher, How Jewish is Christianity?, p. 137; Steve Maltz, To Life!, pp. 183-185.

It is a story of יְהֹוָה Yehovah who repeatedly shows mercy, love, forgiveness and salvation to His people. Kaiser adds,

> 'the priority and absoluteness of God's grace are constantly reiterated.' The [תּוֹרָה Torah], then, must not be viewed as an abstract, impersonal tractate that stands inertly over the heads of men and women. It was, first of all, *intensely personal.*

And the תּוֹרָה Torah "was that which *made living possible.* Without it, people could not live at all."[220] Did you know the תּוֹרָה Torah has more than four times as much to say about mercy than the R.C.?[221] The Psalms, are they 'law' to your ears? תּוֹרָה Torah is our salvation, our life, and our freedom! Here is an interesting quote given by Rabbi Rashi,

> The Torah is much more than a book of laws; it is the legacy of the Jewish people. It tells of the creation of a nation, chosen by God to be His emissaries of kindness, justice, goodness and recognition of the one true Creator. It starts with the creation of the world so that there would be no question that *Eretz Yisrael* belongs to them...[222]

Jerusalem365 once entered this statement:

> The giving of the Torah was the single most important moment in the history of civilization for all of mankind. Long ago, the Sages wondered if

220 Walter Kaiser, Jr., and Kaiser, Toward Old Testament Ethics, 1983, USA, p. 77.

221 Chuck & Karen Cohen, Roots of our Faith, 2002, Jerusalem Publishing, p. 21.

222 Rabbi Rashi as quoted by Rabbi Tuly Weisz, The Israel Bible, p. 4.

the Torah is so holy, why wasn't it given in the Holy Land? The ancient rabbis explained that God chose to transmit His moral code on a barren mountain in the owner-less desert to emphasize that His Word is for everyone equally, because His instructions are the key to universal survival. In the Book of Rut (Ruth) we read about the Moabite Rut who forges her own path to Mount Sinai through her relationship with her mother-in-law Naomi. Rut is associated with the holiday of Shavuot because, with great self-sacrifice, she finds her way to the ultimate truth of the Torah.[223]

May we all take the path of Rut; that is to seek the truth of the תּוֹרָה Torah in relationship to the giver of the תּוֹרָה Torah, the Jews! Here is an important verse Christians often misunderstand. Matthew 5:17, which says, "Don't think I have come to abolish תּוֹרָה Torah or the Prophets. I have come not to abolish but to complete." This verse is often badly translated as: but to fulfil. Young handles this subject well by saying that יֵשׁוּעַ Yeshua loved תּוֹרָה Torah. Often people have said that as יֵשׁוּעַ Yeshua came to fulfil the demands of the Law, and by doing so He rendered it obsolete; He cancelled it for Christians. Young first of all says that in fulfilling the תּוֹרָה Torah and the prophets, יֵשׁוּעַ Yeshua could not also cancel them. On the contrary יֵשׁוּעַ Yeshua is saying that "he seeks to strengthen the Torah through proper interpretation and application." Paul makes a similar remark in Romans 3:31: "Does it follow that we abolish Torah by this trusting? Heaven forbid! On the contrary we confirm Torah." Confirming תּוֹרָה Torah

223 I received from the internet but did not have the date.

"means to interpret the message accurately and to live out the meaning of the text in practice." This passage emphasizes the importance of proper interpretation of תּוֹרָה Torah, as יֵשׁוּעַ Yeshua placed the teaching of תּוֹרָה Torah on a firmer footing. Matthew 5-7 shows us that יֵשׁוּעַ Yeshua is working the תּוֹרָה Torah and interacting with His audience as He teaches them a distinct approach for implementing the ancient precepts for living. Sometimes the interpretation went beyond the plain reading of the text "to reach the highest essence of the divine revelation. It is also an approach that places a premium on even the smallest details of the Torah, neglecting neither *yod* nor *kotz*" (like the dot over the i).[224] יֵשׁוּעַ Yeshua "does not destroy Torah for Christians, he gives Torah fresh meaning through practical application in everyday life." "It is a plan of action."[225] The R.C. instead of being a rejection of the First Covenant it is "rather a renewal and reapplication that blends together a powerful combination of ancient themes and fresh ideas." This makes the תּוֹרָה Torah relevant – fresh life being breathed into the older message but actualizing תּוֹרָה Torah in experience.[226]

So three things are clear. We must stop saying O.T.; refrain from using the word Law for the First Covenant, and see the importance for never neglecting the תּוֹרָה Torah; treating the תּוֹרָה Torah on par with the בְּרִית חֲדָשָׁה Brit Chadashah (R.C.). Stern even advocates that we as Christians can use the word תּוֹרָה Torah to include the

---

224 Young, Meet The Rabbis, pp. 42-47.
225 Ibid., pp. 82, 213.
226 Brad H. Young, The Parables, 1998, USA, p. 30. See also Marvin Wilson, Exploring Our Hebraic Heritage, p. 52.

R.C.[227] Alex Jacob prefers to use the word 'Apostles' when referring to the R.C.. He says that as Luke refers to the early church as giving themselves to the 'Apostle's teaching' (Acts:42), this provides a good title for the final section of the Bible.[228]

'Testament'

Commenting on the word 'Testament' Stern says that this word reflects a tension between the Hebrew language of the Tanakh and the Greek of the **בְּרִית חֲדָשָׁה** B'rit Chadashah. The word B'rit means 'covenant/contract.' But the Greek word employed for 'covenant' has also another meaning – 'testament' in the sense of 'will.' The Hebrew *B'rit Chadashah* has only one meaning – 'renewed *covenant*' whereas the Greek can be translated as 'renewed *testament*.' Jeremiah foretold a renewed covenant "between God and the Jewish people, not a 'will.' – a covenant, not a testament – the term 'New Testament'...obscures the meaning of the original Hebrew '[renewed] Covenant.'" [229] James Whitman adds that the word covenant is code language for God's saving activity. Divine actions in both covenants, is coherent. [230] I certainly agree. There are five covenants made with the Yisra'el,[231] all remaining in force today

227 David Stern, Messianic Jewish Manifesto, 1991, USA, pp. 146-147.

228 Jacob Vince, In Touch mag., (Christian Friends of Israel), 2nd Quarter 2019, No 199, p. 2 and 1st Quarter 2019, No 198, p. 2.

229 Stern, The Complete Bible Study, p. xxx

230 President of The Centre for Judaic-Christian Studies, In Touch mag., 191, p. 6.

231 The Abrahamic, the Levitical, the Davidic, the Mosaic and the Renewed Covenant; Rob Richards, Has God finished with Israel, 2000, UK, pp. 48-49; see also David Evans, Christians & Israel, 2010, p. 28.

(including the Mosaic covenant);[232] the First Covenant and the Renewed Covenant (of Jeremiah 31) (the בְּרִית חֲדָשָׁה B'rit Chadashah) – are all referred to as 'Covenants.' The word 'Testament' can never replace such vocabulary.

Acts 3:21 speaks of a 'restoring of all things.' There are people, myself included, who believe that this includes things that the church forgot or got wrong and then to rediscover truths and attempt to set things right before יֵשׁוּעַ Yeshua returns.

Setting things right – letting the Jewish root support us non-Jews

Sharon Sanders writes,

> ...Now is a time of putting things in order, a time of '*chassidut.*' Israel's sages teach that '*chassidut.*' precedes the coming of the Messiah. They say that preparations for a revelation must precede the revelation as many believe we are living in the time prior to Messiah.
>
> It may be difficult to believe, but as many churches struggle, many synagogues are overflowing. As Christians, we like to say we are 'Torchbearers,' and while this is true, we must come to grips with an embarrassing fact: our forefathers embraced a heretical lie, regarding God's chosen people.

232 David Stern, Messianic Jewish Manifesto, pp. 99-102; Rabbi John Fisher, How Jewish is Christianity?, pp. 130-137; Gershon Nerel, How Jewish is Christianity?, pp. 152-165; Richard E. Averbeck, Israel the Church and the Middle East, Darrell L. Bock and Mitch Glaser, Editors, 2018, USA, pp. 21-37.

(Jeremiah 16:19). The serious offences committed, and the transgressions which resulted from centuries of abuse to the Jewish people by Christianity, requires reparation. Replacement teachings, and Christian anti-Semitism, have resulted in a distressing distrust of Christians, which should make us sick at heart. It is no small matter. Many who live and work in Israel, are involved in the repairing being accomplished here today. *Zion is being restored.*

Yes, our light was blurred to the Chosen Ones. It was the priests of Roman Catholicism who lined up Jewish people during WW11 and gave the command to firing squads, '**Fire in the name of Jesus!**' At the same time, Protestant and Catholic leaders told the Jews, '**Be baptised or die!**' ...As bodies of Jewish people were being torn apart, photos of Christ were hung at the end of torture tables. The last thing a Jew saw was this portrait of Jesus. It was a satanic darkness that came from so-called "Christians." … Arrogance has been a real problem in the Church. We must not be ashamed of the Gospel, but we should be ashamed of what our people did, in the Name of the Lord. Where are our tears?[233]

---

233 Sharon Sanders, For Zion's Sake, Third Quarter, 2018, p. 5. Unfortunately anti-Semitism is still rife in Britain and the West. See Melanie Phillips, The Spectator, Feb. 16, 2002, entitled 'Christians who hate the Jews.' It was noted that the real reason for the antipathy to Israel was the ancient hatred of Jews rooted in Christian theology and simply "rooted in **a dislike of the Jews**." Steve Maltz, The People of Many Names, pp. 142-143.

Maltz asks a question that touches on this subject.

> *What has the modern Western Church mostly got wrong about [Yeshua]?* It's a fair question as there must be some fallout from the 1900 years of Greek thinking in the established Church. The unavoidable fact has to be that the identity and full context of our Saviour had been clouded and hidden from Christians ever since the Roman State Church took a chainsaw to the Olive Tree (Romans 11) and massacred the lower branches and root.[234]

Christians then have a lot of catching up to do. For a start we should repent of this past and do all we can to be better examples of יֵשׁוּעַ love. שֶׁהֲרֵי הַיְשׁוּעָה מֵאֵת הַיְּהוּדִים Salvation is from the Jews[235] (John 4:22) and this includes being taught by Jewish scholarship! The root supports us non-Jews, not the other way around. It's time to humble ourselves.

Sanders continues,

> Some Christian leaders find it unacceptable to learn from Jewish Bible Scholars. They say with pride, and with eyes seeing red, 'how could they (the Jews) teach us (Christians) anything? They don't have

---

234 Steve Maltz, Hebraic Church, p. 82.

235 יֵשׁוּעַ Yeshua was referring to Genesis 49:8-10 which obviously has not been fulfilled yet. Many people think this only applies to יֵשׁוּעַ Yeshua's death and resurrection, His saving us from sin, but the above verse shows this to be a grave fallacy and undue limitation to the meaning of John 4:22. The saying is actually 'loaded' with meaning deserving a book all on its own. See Eli Lizorkin-Eyzenberg, The Jewish Gospel of John, p. 56.

> Jesus!' [But if only] Christians could experience the depth of understanding that many Jewish scholars have, they might join the Pastor who sadly told us, 'I've been preaching for 25 years and I can't hold a candle to the Jews, compared to the knowledge they have of the Bible!' The Jewish people have been terribly misjudged, and presumed spiritually dead.[236]
>
> It is time to get rid of long-time dogmatic teachings that are not Scriptural...At a time of rising anti-Semitism across Europe and even North America, it is...essential that steps be taken to defend the integrity of Judaism and its sacred texts...[237]

As Israel continues to find יֵשׁוּעַ Yeshua, God's blessing will flow – so keep your eyes peeled for the new Jewish books/magazines coming out. I highly recommend the books written by Brad Young, Nehemiah Gordon, Marvin Wilson, Chuck Cohen, David Bivin, Roy Blizzard, Lois Tverberg, Arnold Fruchtenbaum (especially 'Israelology: The Missing Link in Systematic Theology), Steve Maltz, and David Stern. Some magazines I recommend are, for instance, Israel Today, Israel My Glory, In Touch, For Zion's Sake (and there are plenty more).

Stern now adds something that most people have overlooked. There is a deeper reason for paying attention to Judaism – Ephesians 2:11-13, 19-20. In particular vs 12,

236 Sharon Sanders, For Zion's Sake, Third Quarter, 2018, pp. 5-6.
237 Sharon Sanders, For Zion's Sake, Fourth Quarter, 2017, p. 5 col. 2 & 3.

> at the time [you] had no Messiah. You were estranged from the national life of Isra'el. You were foreigners to the covenants embodying God's promise... vs 19, So then you are no longer foreigners and strangers. On the contrary, you are fellow-citizens with God's people and members of God's family. Vs 20, You have been built up on the foundation of the emissaries and the prophets, with the cornerstone being Yeshua Messiah himself.

God's people, God's family, the emissaries, the prophets and יֵשׁוּעַ Yeshua – who are they but the Jews. These verses tells us that Gentiles were separate from Christ, excluded from citizenship in Israel and foreigners to the covenants. So when a Gentile puts his faith in יֵשׁוּעַ Yeshua, God then makes these Gentiles part of the people of God, the Jews! יֵשׁוּעַ Yeshua then welcomes them to participate in the Jewish covenants. Yes, in effect Christianity is nothing more than a Messianic branch of Judaism. As Stern asks:

> How many churches teach that the Messiah's *first* gift to Gentile believers in him is *inclusion in the national life of Israel* – which is to say, the national life of the Jewish people (or, as the Kings James version puts it, the 'commonwealth of Israel.')? How many Christians embrace the Jewish people fully – or even tentatively? Very few. Is this point made in any creed? Not that I know of. In fact, very few Gentile Christians even know that they have been brought into the national life of Israel, that by faith in Yeshua they are inseparably and eternally joined to the Jewish people. That is what Ephesians 3:4-6 means. There [Sha'ul] explains, '...how I

> understand this secret plan concerning the Messiah. In past generations it was not made known to mankind as the Spirit is now revealing it to his emissaries and prophets, that in union with the Messiah and through the Good News the Gentiles were to be *joint heirs, a joint body and joint sharers with the Jews in what God had promised*.

Stern further brings out another neglected point.

> The creeds include the fact that Yeshua is the Son of God and the second person of the Trinity, but does any creed mention that he is King of the Jews? Instead, throughout most of its existence the church has taught that Christians have *not* joined up with the people of Israel, the Jewish people, but have *replaced* them and *become Israel themselves*![238]

Our creeds and confessions are outdated! I'm not saying that we need to totally abandon them but they could be updated and added to. Some of the wording is very archaic and some words are plain wrong.[239] As far as I know all the creeds were made in the spirit of anti-Semitism and is why I believe that all the creeds are anti-Semitic, not in what they say particularly, but in what they omit. The fact that Rabbis were not invited in the process to help form

---

238 David H. Stern, Restoring The Jewishness of the Gospel, 2009, Jewish New Testament Publications, pp. 73-75 and How Jewish is Christianity?, p. 190.

239 For example the phrase 'Only begotten' which is from Psalm 82. The confusing translation of monogenes which does not mean 'birthing' as this actually contradicts scripture. Greek scholars realize now there was a mistake in translation and actually means 'one of a kind' or 'unique.' Heiser, The Unseen Realm, pp. 36-37.

decisions speaks a lot.[240] Many years ago my Philosophy professor stressed church creeds and confessions should never be rigid in time but updated to the needs of the congregates in each century. If we are to make use of creeds then, for instance I would include, as other churches have, that because of the onslaught of evolution on our society, church creeds could include something about a young creation as taught in scripture. I would also include something about marriage as being between one man and one woman. And now we see of course that we need to make statements about our beliefs concerning the Jews.

So then, us non-Jews are no longer to be foreigners and strangers but fellow-citizens with God's holy people and members of God's holy family, the Jewish people. In short "the more biblical one becomes, the more Semitic one will be."[241] In Galatians 3:29 we are reminded that if we belong to יֵשׁוּעַ Yeshua, we are the seed of Avraham. According to this we see that Christianity begins with father Avraham.

Wilson comments,

> The question of who joins whom ought to be of vital interest to every Christian. Some Christians teach that Israel and the church are not two separate entities but that God's will is to eliminate that

---

240 See Steve Maltz, How The Church Lost The Truth, p. 77 and To Life!, 2011, UK, pp. 96, 100-101, 171-172. Maltz shows the difference in Hebraic thought verses Greek thinking in relation to creeds and how this lead to Christianity becoming a philosophical system. Viola and Barna also show how Greek philosophy "has always been fond of creedal statements and doctrinal statements" - Frank Viola and George Barna, Pagan Christianity, p. 204.

241 Wilson, Our Father Abraham, p. 20.

> distinction by having Israel convert to Christianity and join the church. The ultimate conclusion of such teaching would of course be the disappearance of Israel. The apostle Paul, however, has a different answer to this question of who joins whom...Paul argues that non-Jewish believers are grafted in the olive tree, Israel (Rom. 11:11-24). Through the use of this metaphor of the olive tree, Paul depicts non-Jewish believers as wild olive branches. Gentiles are not 'natural' branches but 'wild.' Thus God, by his mercy, graciously grafts them into Israel. Accordingly, non-Jews are allowed to partake of the rich sap derived from the root of the olive tree, that faith-filled channel of spiritual nourishment found in Abraham and his descendants. In this way non-Jews join the remnant of the Jewish people. But Halvor Ronning is correct in pointing out that 'even the secular Jews must be accepted as somehow a part of the family. However problematic it may seem, we gain some kind of special relationship even to them.' Thus the biblical answer of who joins whom is clear: we non-Jewish believers, formerly excluded from partnership with Israel, are joined to Israel in this divinely ordained olive tree connection (Rom. 11:24). In short, Israel is the people we join.[242]

There are a number of scholars that would say,

> ...the Gentiles' future in relationship to Israel is that they will either be 'subdued by Israel and

242 Wilson, Exploring Our Hebraic Heritage, p. 66; see also his book Our Father Abraham, pp. 19-20, 22.

> compelled to serve Israel,' or they will be converted 'to the faith of Israel so as to serve Israel's God.' In the eschatological future, 'Israel remains the people of God, and the future salvation is first of all Israel's salvation.'[243]

Christians would do well to observe what Rut did. Rut knew the above truth and so cried out, **עַמֵּךְ עַמִּי וֵאלֹהַיִךְ אֱלֹהָי** "Your people are my people and your God is my God" (Rut 1:16). People tend to remember her words "your God is my God" but forget she also said "**Your people are my people**." As a Gentile, she first binds herself for life to the nation and people of Israel and *only then* receives the God of the Jews.[244]

> Christians must learn...that in Yeshua they become part of a great big Jewish family, and it is within this family relationship that they find God, along with his covenants, promises and hope. This is what is meant by the olive tree metaphor of Romans 11:17-24, which says that Gentile 'wild branches' have been grafted into God's olive tree (the Jewish people[245]) among the natural branches (the Jews). What is spoken here is not mystical but practical. Through the faith in the Jewish Messiah a Gentile can have God-enhanced, God-blessed human

243 Arnold G. Fruchtenbaum, Israelology: The Missing Link In Systematic Theology, p. 245.

244 Stern, Restoring The Jewishness of the Gospel, p. 76; see also Stern, The Complete Jewish Study Bible, p. 1191.

245 C.E.B. Cranfield, Romans 9-16 commentary, pp. 564-565; Stern, Jewish New Testament Commentary, p. 413; and David Bivin, New Light on the Words of Jesus, p. 149; Arnold G. Fruchtenbaum, Israelology: The Missing Link In Systematic Theology, pp. 743-745; Wilson, Our Father Abraham, p. 15.

> relationships with Jews and with other Gentiles who have found Yeshua and accept him as the atonement for their sins, as well as with Jews who haven't yet accepted him.
>
> If Jews fail to welcome Christians as 'Family,' it's not the fault of the Jews but the fault of Christians who do not understand who they are in Messiah Yeshua! And it therefore becomes the Christians' responsibility to re-think their identity so that they can do whatever will be necessary to undo centuries of misunderstanding between Jews and Christians and ultimately to make real their closeness and identification with the Jewish people.[246]

Rabbi Tuly Weisz reminds us that we have, "the creation of a people [Israel], the nation chosen by Hashem[247] to be His representatives in the world and to carry out His mission of being a light to the nations,"[248] – this calling has not changed for 4000 years.[249] As Christians our calling is to join them. Romans 9:4-5 "is speaking of Israel's national adoption (Exod. 4:22) by which Israel became the national son of God...Israel was never disinherited from that position (Isa. 63:16; Jer. 3:17-19, 31:9, 20)."[250] In addition Fruchtenbaum says (Romans 11:1), "The fact that Paul

---

246 Stern, Restoring The Jewishness of the Gospel, p. 76. See also Chuck & Karen Cohen, Roots of our Faith, pp. 222, 229.

247 Another name for God.

248 Rabbi Tuly Weisz, The Israel Bible, p. 3.

249 See also Eli Lizorkin-Eyzenberg, The Jewish Gospel of John, where he shows this clearly throughout his commentary and Richard E. Averbeck, Israel the Church and the Middle East, pp. 29, 35-36; Gershon Nerel, How Jewish is Christianity?, pp. 102-103.

250 Arnold G. Fruchtenbaum, Israelology: The Missing Link In Systematic Theology, p. 727; see also 709.

refers to Israel as *his* people in the present age shows that they are still the chosen people."[251] So let us join the chosen people. Christians are also chosen, but not as rivals. I believe the Jewishness of the gospel is stripped out of today's sermons when pastors just say "we are now adopted" or "we are now in God's family"; adopted into what? And what family? The answer is that we are adopted into a Jewish family – Jewish brothers and sisters.[252] Why cannot we be proud of that.

> Rut...answers the call in one of the most beautiful statements of faith and allegiance in the entire Bible. Her words and actions set her on a path of royalty, and have inspired the faithful for hundreds of years. Rut demonstrates for all time what it means to cast one's lot with the people of Israel, the Land of Israel and the God of Israel. For Rut's sacrifice, she was rewarded by becoming the matriarch of the Davidic dynasty, and the ancestress of the Mashiach.[253]

The natural branches (Jewish people) are rooted in Jewish festivals,[254] Jewish community and the Jewish Messiah.[255] That's where we are rooted and let us rejoice in that root. Though the historical issues are more complex, A. J. Heschel insightfully described a problem:

---

251 Ibid., p. 740, also see pp. 744-745, 819.

252 See David H. Stern, Messianic Jewish Manifesto, 1991, pp. 42-51.

253 Weisz, The Israel Bible, p. 1800.

254 Another interesting aspect of joining the Jewish people is participating in their festivals. Many books are available on this subject. When 'reliving' these rich festivals with Messianic Jews you get to learn and feel the connection they have in the Messiah which we non-Jews have lost.

255 Merril Bolender, p. 19.

> The process of dejudaization within the church paved the way for abandonment of origins and alienation from the core of its message. The vital issue for the church is to decide whether to look for roots in Judaism and consider itself an extension of Judaism or to look for roots in pagan Hellenism and consider itself as an antithesis to Judaism.[256]

> If a fellowship has issues with the Jewish people, or consciously avoids the subject, then they have a serious issue with God. If you didn't know this before, then you know it now.[257]

Have all things been fulfilled in Christ?

Christians often say 'all things are fulfilled in Christ.' That is a meaningless statement. No one has or could go through the whole תּוֹרָה Torah and research all prophesy to see if all has been fulfilled in Christ. If it was, hopefully, many of us would be in heaven right now! No – through Christ everything **will be eventually** fulfilled; but at present absolutely not. We haven't even had the rapture, tribulation, Armageddon, or the thousand year reign yet. Stern says it this way, "He is the instrument through whom God the Father has fulfilled, is fulfilling and will fulfil every promise he has ever made..."[258]

The importance of the Covenants

Fruchtenbaum begins by saying that the Davidic covenant (11 Samuel 7:11b-16) promises that David will be head of

256 A. J. Heschel, as quoted by Brad H. Young, The Parables, p. 28.
257 Steve Maltz, Hebraic Church, p. 210.
258 Stern, Messianic Jewish Manifesto, pp. 111-112.

a dynasty and that the Davidic Kingdom will be eternal (vs 16). The emphasis of 1 Chronicles 17:10b-14 is on the Messiah, who will build the Millennial Temple, and His throne will be established forever. Here יֵשׁוּעַ Yeshua will function as king which begins at the second coming (see also Psalm 89, Isaiah 9:6-7, and Jeremiah 23:22). Jeremiah 33:22 says the seed of David will multiply exceedingly (see also Ezekiel 37:1-23) and vs 23-26 says this is to prove those wrong who say that God no longer intends to fulfil His covenants with His Holy people. But יְהוָה will fulfil every promise of the covenants. Amos 9:11-12 speaks of the ruins of David to be repaired and David's throne will exercise all the glory of previous days extending over the Gentile nations. Luke 1:32-35 clarifies that יְהוָה Yehovah gives יֵשׁוּעַ Yeshua the eternal throne of David.[259]

Now here it gets interesting:

> For Adonai will have compassion on Ya'akov – he will once again choose Yisra'el and resettle them in their own land [began pre-1948 to today], where foreigners will join them, attaching themselves to the house of Ya'akov. Peoples will take and escort them to their homeland, [which is certainly happening today] and the house of Yisra'el will possess them in the land of Adonai as male and female slaves. They will take their captors captive and rule over their oppressors (Isaiah 14:1-2).

Non-Jews will be possessed one day by the Jewish nation. Similarly, Isaiah 49:22-23 informs us that the Gentiles will

259 Fruchtenbaum, Israelology: The Missing Link In Systematic Theology, pp. 803-806.

assist in aiding the Jews back into the land. But not only that, we will become the servants of the Jewish people.

> I am beckoning to the nations, raising my banner for the peoples. They will bring your sons in their arms and carry your daughters on their shoulders. Kings will be your foster-fathers, their princes your nurses. They will bow to you, face toward the earth, and lick the dust on your feet. Then you will know that I am Adonai... (Isaiah 49:22-23).

According to Isaiah 60:1-3, the reason Israel will become the centre of Gentile attention is due to the fact that the Shechinah Glory will abide over Israel.

According to Isaiah 61:4-9, when the regathering takes place, Israel will rebuild all the desolate cities of the land (v.4). At that time, the Gentiles will become the servants to Israel and will feed the flocks and plow the fields (v. 5). As for Israel, they will be the ministers of the Word to the Gentiles (v. 6a) and will receive the wealth of the Gentiles for their enjoyment (v.6b). Israel will never again be shamed by the Gentiles, but rather they will receive a double portion of all the blessings and possessions (v. 7). This will be the result of the [Renewed] covenant (v.8). The Jews will be known among the Gentiles, and all the Gentiles will acknowledge that it is the Jews who have been especially chosen by God for special blessings (v. 9).

Isaiah's contemporary, Micah, also had something to say in this regard in Micah 7:14-17. Israel is to be regathered in order to possess the land (v.14),

> and this regathering will be accomplished by miracles (v. 15). When the Gentiles see this, they will cease reproaching the Jews and will have a reverential fear of the Jews. They will then submit to the God of Israel (vv. 16-17.[260]

Which one of our creeds mentions this! It is so important that we know what Isaiah (along with other prophets) is saying because if you look closely his words are being fulfilled before our eyes!

> Strangers will stand and feed your flocks, foreigners plow your land and tend your vines; but you will be called *cohanim* [priests] of Adonai, spoken of as ministers to our God. You will feed on the wealth of the nations, and revel in their riches. Because of your shame, which was doubled, and because they cried, 'They deserve disgrace,' therefore in their land what they own will be doubled, and joy forever will be theirs (Isaiah 61:5-7).

The Jews will be the ministers of the Word of יְהוָה Yehovah to the Gentiles. Now we have it – Jews will be teaching us, not the other way around. And the Jews will receive the wealth of the nations – the wealth from us Gentiles. Given the prominence of Israel, when was the last time your fellowship has given a gift to Israel? This is the result of the Renewed Covenant (vs 8) that all non-Jews will finally acknowledge that it is the Jews who have been

260 Ibid., p. 807.

chosen by יְהוָה Yehovah for special blessings.[261] When Gentiles can't see the connection between the land of Yisra'el today and prophesy, they either don't understand prophesy or the meaning of miracles.[262] Every war Yisra'el has had, and they have sadly experienced many, they have been severely outnumbered, sometimes almost 100 to one in planes, tanks, ammunition, and soldiers – they were not pushed into the sea for one reason only: the miracles of יְהוָה Yehovah's saving power.[263] God will make the Jews an object of fame and praise among us Gentiles (Zephaniah 3:20). They will become the centre of our attention, so much so, that ten men will grab hold of the cloak of a Jew and say, "we want to go with you, because we have heard that God is with you." (Zechariah 8:20-21).[264] It is now time to be God's hands and feet, to play into God's purposes for Israel; to begin blessing the Jews.

Deuteronomy 15:6 says,

> Yes, Adonai your God will bless you, as he promised you – you will lend money to many nations without having to borrow, and you will rule over many nations without their ruling over you.

---

261 Fruchtenbaum, Israelology: The Missing Link In Systematic Theology, p. 807.

262 For those who would like to see the connection, I recommend Lance Lambert, The Uniqueness of Israel, 1984, UK or Hugh Kitson, Jerusalem the Covenant City, 2000, UK.

263 See Chaim Herzog, The Arab-Israeli Wars, 1992, UK or Lance Lambert, Battle For Israel, 1988, UK.

264 It is interesting that King Louis XIV of France asked Blaise Pascal for a proof of the existence of God and Pascal immediately replied,"The Jews, your majesty." Steve Maltz, How The Church Lost The Way, p. 163.

And 28:13, "Adonai will make you the head and not the tail; and you will be only above, never below..." It was a fact that Yisra'el was to become the head of the Gentiles when Yisra'el received their national regeneration (see also as previously mentioned, Isaiah 49:22-23 and 61:6-7). [265] Based on these Scriptures we can see that God is bringing Gentiles into the place of blessing. These blessing are based on the Jewish covenants. Fruchtenbaum believes the Olive tree (Romans 11:16-24) represents the place of spiritual blessing rooted in the Abrahamic Covenant. The same points made in Ephesians2:11-16 and 3:5-6 are saying we become partakers of the Jewish spiritual blessings. We do not take-over these blessings, we partake.[266]

Who does יֵשׁוּעַ Yeshua represent?

Stern explains by saying one way

> to think about the Gospel as simultaneously individual and corporate is to consider the ways in which the Messiah Yeshua stands for and is intimately identified with His people [Yisra'el]. Just as the individual who trusts Yeshua becomes united with him and is 'immersed' (baptised) into all that Yeshua is, including his death and resurrection – so that his sin nature is regarded as dead, and his new nature...is regarded as alive – just as this intimate identification with the Messiah holds for the individual, so the Messiah similarly

265 Fruchtenbaum, Israelology: The Missing Link In Systematic Theology, p. 808.

266 Ibid., pp. 743-745. This idea is also seen in the commentary of Weisz's Israel Bible, p. 902.

> identifies with and embodies national [Yisra'el]. In the [R.C.] one encounters this notion first at Mattityahu [Matthew] 2:15, where it is said of Yeshua's being taken into Egypt, 'This happened in order to fulfill what Adonai had said through the prophet, 'Out of Egypt I called my son.' The verse quoted is Hosea 11:1. However in context the prophet Hosea was clearly speaking not about a future Messiah but about the nation of [Yisra'el] and the Exodus.[267]
>
> Mattityahu...is giving us a *remez*, a hint of a very deep truth. [Yisra'el] is called God's son as far back as Exodus 4:22. The Messiah is presented as God's son a few verses earlier in Mattityahu 1:18-25, reflecting Tanakh passages such as Isaiah 9:6-7, Psalm 2:7 and Proverbs 30:4. Thus the Son equals the son; the Messiah is equated with the nation of Yisra'el. This is what Mattityahu is hinting at by calling Yeshua's flight to Egypt a 'fulfilment' of Hosea 11:1.[268]

The idea that יֵשׁוּעַ Yeshua stands for Yisra'el can be found throughout the Bible.[269] In the Isaiah passage of 49:1-6,

> he has said, 'Is it not enough that you are merely my servant to raise up the tribes of Ya'akov and

267 Stern, Messianic Jewish Manifesto, pp. 105-106.

268 Stern, Messianic Jewish Manifesto, p. 107. See also his commentary, pp. 12-13. See also James Whitman, In Touch mag., (Christian Friends of Israel), 2nd Quarter 2018, No 195, p. 4.

269 Stern gives these examples: Joshua 7, 1Kings 9:3-9, Romans 5:12-21, 1 Corinthians 15:45-49, Isaiah 42:1-9, 49:1-13, 50:4-11, 52:11-53:12. See also Frank Viola, Insurgence, 2018, USA, pp, 99-100.

> restore the offspring of [Yisra'el]. I will also make you a light to the nations, so my salvation can spread to the ends of the earth.'

Stern asks,

> Does Yisra'el restore the preserved of Yisra'el? Who is the 'light to the nations'? Judaism understands this as a goal to be fulfilled by the Jewish people. Christians think at once of Yochanan [John] 8:12, where Yeshua said of himself, 'I am the light of the world.' I suggested at the beginning...that the Jewish people will be the light to the nations that we ought to be when we have in us him who is the light of the world.[270]

John MacArthur and Richard Mayhue agree saying that יֵשׁוּעַ Yeshua,

> the true [Yisra'el], will restore the nation Israel and bring light to the nations...this means that Israel, who was given a mission to the nations, will be able to accomplish its mission because of the Servant [Yeshua].[271]

Likewise, Roy H. Schoeman comments,

> The fact that the Messiah is the eternal Son of God made flesh is also a metonymy: he is Israel not by substitution, but by inclusion. He is the one in

---

270 Stern, Messianic Jewish Manifesto, pp. 107-108.

271 John MacArthur and Richard Mayhue, Christ's Prophetic Plans, 2012, USA, p. 113.

whom the filial condition of the holy nation is realized.[272]

The Israel "par excellence."[273] Kelvin Crombie adds,

> [Yeshua's] circumcision confirmed Him as part of the covenant with Abraham. He would carry on His body the physical sign of that covenant which could not be removed, revealing His identity according to the flesh – a sign that he was part of the nation of Israel." "...[Yeshua] was indeed destined for a very important task – to be a light to the Gentiles AND to be the glory of God's covenant nation Israel.[274]

Stern continues,

> This concept, that the Messiah embodies the Jewish people, should not seem strange to believers, who learn precisely that about Yeshua and the Church. What else does it mean to talk of the Church as a body of which the Messiah is the head? Or a temple of which he is the cornerstone? The concept of one standing for all is familiar. But the Church has not clearly grasped that the Holy One of [Yisra'el], Yeshua, is in union not only with the Church, but also with the Jewish people. When Christians have fully digested this and can communicate to Jews that through Yeshua the Messiah, by virtue of his identification with Israel, the Jewish people will achieve their destiny, then the Jewish people will

272 Roy H. Schoeman, Salvation is from the Jews, 2003, USA, p. 325.

273 Donald Guthrie as cited by Michael Rydelnil, Israel the Church and the Middle East, p. 80.

274 Kelvin Crombie, Israel, Jesus and Covenant, pp. 205-206.

> have been presented a less alien and more attractive Gospel. And the Church will have become faithful to it.
>
> 'The truth, the whole truth, and nothing but the truth'? Yeshua said, 'I am...the truth.' But he identifies with [Yisra'el]. A believer in the Gospel acquires truth by identifying with Yeshua. But if so, he too, whether Jewish of Gentile, must identify with the Jewish people, with whom Yeshua identifies. Otherwise he has not identified with Yeshua. That's the truth! 'Ye shall know the truth' – Yeshua, who identifies with the Jewish people – 'and the truth shall make you free.'[275]

It concerns me that in most churches I doubt that most people know **יֵשׁוּעַ** Yeshua is in fact a Jew. Pastors should survey their fellowships to see if different age groups actually know this. If I am correct, then why not call **יֵשׁוּעַ** Yeshua Rabbi or Rabbi **יֵשׁוּעַ** Yeshua occasionally, as this might help drive the point?

Non-Jewish vs Jewish hermeneutics

One obstacle Christians are going to have to overcome is the whole concept of Jewish hermeneutics. The more I study Jewish insights into scripture the clearer it is that there is a deficiency of the Western grammatical-historical exegesis. Jacob Prasch contends,

275 Stern, Messianic Jewish Manifesto, p. 108. See also, Steve Maltz, To Life, chapter 13.

Western grammatico-historical interpretation[276] is all well and good, but from the perspective of first century [Judaism] I contend it is right in what it confirms yet is wrong in what it omits. It allows people to see the basic truth and as such pointed people back to the gospel. The grammatico-historical approach focused on many important things, such as the literal meaning of the text, context, induction over deduction, exegesis (interpretation of the biblical text) over *eisegesis* (reading something into a biblical text not there). And so on, and the essentials of this approach are correct. But it did not travel far enough down the road towards restoring a first century Jewish-Christian hermeneutic.

Let me put it this way: if you work in a corner shop, you only need arithmetic; if you want to be a rocket scientist, you need calculus. Both arithmetic and calculus are mathematics, but the latter takes the discipline of mathematics much farther. Likewise, if you want to understand, say, properly apocalyptic literature in the Bible, you cannot limit a study of it to the grammatico-historical approach. Quite simply, you will never fully understand Jewish...literature if you only interpret it with the linguistic and historical tools of grammatico-historical interpretation. Something more is needed, which some people began to realize some time after the Reformation.[277]

276 Or 'grammatical-historical exegesis.'

277 Jacob Prasch, The Jews, Modern Israel and the New Supersessionism, pp. 194-195.

In Judaism there are four basic modes of Scripture interpretation used by the Rabbis. These are: 1) P'shat (simple) – the plain, literal sense of the text, similar to what we call the grammatical-historical exegesis. The grammar and historical setting helps decide what a passage means. Modern Non-Jewish interpreters often consider only this method as valid. 2) Remez (hint) – a word, phrase or another element hints at a truth (not seen with the p'shat). It is presupposed that God can hint at things that the Bible authors themselves may not have been aware. 3) Drash or midrash (search) – an allegorical or homiletical application to the text (involving eisegesis as well as exegesis). The presupposition is that the words of Scripture can legitimately become 'grist for the mill' (anything that can be turned to profit or advantage) of human intellect, which God can guide to truths not directly related to the text. 4) Sod (secret) – a hidden meaning obtained by using the numerical values of the Hebrew letters, noticing any unusual spellings, transposing letters etc.. It is presupposed that God invests meaning in the minutest details of the תּוֹרָה Torah. These methods express God's omnipotence and love for all humanity, using extraordinary means to reach people's hearts and minds. Stern believes that it is an overreaction by modern scholars to ignore the other modes of exegesis because of the abuse of grossly over-allegorizing scripture by the church fathers. This error probably came about from their misunderstanding the limitations of, and misusing, the other Rabbinic methods of interpretation. But the R.C. "is a Jewish book, written by Jews in a Jewish context; and the first-century Jewish context included all four ways of handling the text."[278] The four methods listed above are known in Hebrew as *pardes*, meaning 'orchard and Steve Maltz well demonstrates how יֵשׁוּעַ Yeshua used all these methods.[279]

Wilson informs us that

> Biblical teachings are further developed, commented on, and explicated for daily living in the Hebrew prophets and in other later sources such as the Mishnah, Talmud, and Codes.
>
> If the withered or rotted roots of today's church are to become revived through a new understanding of the church's Hebraic beginnings, the church must nourish itself from the sources, those central documents vital to Hebraic thought and life that have shaped Judaism over the centuries.[280]

The largest and most significant written material from the time of Yeshua is known as 'Rabbinic Literature.' The best known is the Mishnah.[281] What are Mishnah, Talmud, and Codes? A fundamental principle in Judaism is that when Moses came down Mt. Sinai, he received not just the

---

278 Stern, Jewish New Testament Commentary, pp. 11-12 and The Jewish Manifesto, pp. 106-107. The Christian theologian Karl Barth also supports these modes of exegesis, Ibid., p. 13.

279 Steve Maltz, How The Church Lost The Way, pp. 75-82. His book, To Life!, pp. 145-147 offers a very good example of how Jewish scholars would use pardes. Maltz is a Jewish believer in יֵשׁוּעַ Yeshua and his books are well worth reading. See also Dr. Ron Moseley, Yeshua, pp. 128-129.

280 Marvin Wilson, Exploring Our Hebraic Heritage, p. 38.

281 David Bivin and Roy Blizzard, Understanding the Difficult Words of Jesus, p. 43.

written תּוֹרָה Torah (called Mikra – that which is read) but also the non-written Torah called the תּוֹרָה שֶׁבְּעַל פֶּה (or הֲלָכָה [282]) Oral Torah (often called by Gentiles the Oral Law but remember Law now is a ditched term) referred to as the Mishnah – that which is repeated. Support for this concept came from Leviticus 26:46: "These are the וְהַתּוֹרֹת laws, ruling and teachings that יְהֹוָה himself gave to the people of יִשְׂרָאֵל Yisra'el on Mount Sinai through Moses." תּוֹרָה Torah was in the plural and this was interpreted as the two laws mentioned at Mount Sinai. The Oral תּוֹרָה Torah, the Mishnah was also memorized being past down from generation to generation. The Mishnah (plural is midrashim) was to help preserve the relevance and application of the Written *תּוֹרָה* Torah. It clarified issues not explained in the Written תּוֹרָה Torah. For example, the written תּוֹרָה Torah says that צִיצִת Tzitziyot [283] were to be worn on their garments (Numbers 15:37); the Oral תּוֹרָה Torah likewise explains how this is to be be carried out. This can be said of all other laws in the Tanach.[284] In יֵשׁוּעַ day, these two Torahs were viewed as תּוֹרָה Torah. Our English/Western Greek and Hellenistic mindset struggles to comprehend that it is these two Torah's that יֵשׁוּעַ Yeshua is giving fresh meaning to for practical application in everyday life. It is true that יֵשׁוּעַ Yeshua and Paul drew their teaching from the oral traditions of the sages as well as the Scriptures, all under the guidance of the Holy Spirit. The Mishnah was never intended to be written down but nevertheless between

---

282 Melissa Briggs, In Touch mag., (Christian Friends of Israel), 1st Quarter 2019, No 198, p. 8.

283 See Rabbi Adin Even-Israel Steinsaltz, Reference Guide to the Talmud, p. 444 and Phylacteries תְּפִילִּין p. 445.

284 Chaim Pearl & Reuben Brookes, A Guide to Jewish Knowledge, 1958, UK, p. 105.

200-350 it was and developed into the Talmud (that which is studied). The Gemara is a commentary on the Mishnah. There are also the Tosefta which are additions to and commentary on the Mishnah. The Gemara together with the Mishnah, is known as the Talmud. The Jewish community in Jerusalem produced the Jerusalem Talmud and the Jewish community in Babylon produced the larger Babylonian Talmud (the Babylonian Talmud gaining the most authority). Then there are the minor tractates of the Talmud numbering around fifteen books concerning life events like marriage, comforting those that mourn, writing **תּוֹרָה** Torah scrolls and manners and custom etc..[285] There are other Rabbinic works, including midrashic (a loosely affiliated group of early Jewish exegetical and homiletical commentaries on the Tanakh) and the Targums (the various Aramaic Translations or paraphrases of the Tanakh).[286] Some of these works are translated into English,[287] but unfortunately most of us would not be expected to be able to read this material, even if we had the time. That is why it

---

285 Nehemiah Gordon, The Hebrew Yeshua vs. the Greek Jesus, pp. 11-13; Brad H. Young, Meet The Rabbis, pp. 81-87, 89; Roy B. Blizzard, Mishnah and the Words of Jesus, 2013, USA, pp. 8-12; Marvin Wilson, Exploring Our Hebraic Heritage, p.46; David Stern, The Complete Jewish Study Bible, p. xiii; Herbert Danby, The Mishnah, 2016 (4th printing), pp. xiii-xiv, xvii; Richard Bank, The Everything JUDAISM BOOK, pp. 52-58; Chaim Pearl & Reuben Brookes, A Guide to Jewish Knowledge, 1958, UK, pp. 65-66; Rabbi Adin Even-Israel Steinsaltz, Reference Guide to the Talmud, pp. 89-95.

286 Stern, The Complete Jewish Study Bible, p. xiv.

287 Stern, The Complete Jewish Study Bible recommends, p. xiv (all are available from Hendrickson Publishers): Danby Herbert, The Mishnah; Jacob, ed. Neusner, The Babylonian and Jerusalem Talmuds; Jacob Neusner, The Tosefta. Young, Meet the Rabbis, p. 82, promotes in addition: Philip Blackman, a multi-volume edition of the Mishnah (includes Hebrew text); Rabbi Adin Even-Israel Steinsaltz has just released 'The Steinsaltz Humash (Humash are the Five books of Moses), Koren Publishers.

is imperative to allow those who have, to help inform out theology.

For instance, here is a good example of learning from our Jewish brothers where they are entrusted with the very words of יְהֹוָה Yehovah. "What advantage has the Jew?...Much in every way! In the first place, they were entrusted with the very words of God"[288] In Genesis 12:3 we read,

> I will make of you a great nation, I will bless you, and I will make your name great; and you are to be a blessing. I will bless those who bless you, but I will curse anyone who curses you; and by you all the families of the earth will be blessed.

Bless is made of three characters ברך. To kneel is בָּרַךְ and is by implication to bless יְהֹוָה Yehovah (as an act of adoration). From this word we get בֶּרֶךְ Berech: a knee. Bless in Hebrew is also an agricultural term (from knee) meaning to graft. This is in the Talmud. So 'will be blessed' is a term of grafting. Genesis 12:3 could read, 'in you and your descendants all the families of the earth will be grafted.' Could Paul have had this in mind when he talked about grafting? (Romans 11:17-19).[289] Did you also notice the sentence, 'I will curse anyone who curses you' and in conection with Matthew 24-25, Rabbi Barney Kasdan counselled,

288 Romans 3:1-2.

289 Nehemia Gordon, Minding Your Own Business, YouTube July 7, 2014.; see also Strong's Concordance.

…The parable emphasizes that one of the best fruits of salvation for non-Jews will actually be their treatment of the Jewish people in their daily lives. Since the days of Abraham, God has given both promise and warning regarding how the Nations treat Israel (cf. Genesis 12:1-3). Clearly, the fruit of one's salvation may be evident in many ways, but it is reasonable that the proper treatment of God's *own* people will be a direct manifestation of that fruit.[290]

The Oral Torah

Stern well knows the importance of the Oral **תּוֹרָה** Torah, so I will let him defend it.

> The common Christian idea that Judaism became 'degenerate' because human tradition was added to God's Law is mistaken. The five books of Moses have rightly been called the constitution of the Jewish nation, but a nation needs more than a constitution. There could never had been a time when tradition of some sort was not a necessary adjunct the written *Torah* – for the written *Torah* simply does not contain all the laws and customs needed to run a nation.
>
> For this there is evidence even in the Pentateuch. Moses wrote in Deuteronomy 12:21 that the people of Israel could slaughter animals 'as I have commanded you,' but no commands concerning how to slaughter are found anywhere in the written

290 Rabbi Barney Kasdan, A Messianic Commentary on Matthew, 2011, USA, p. 325; see also Stern, Messianic Jewish Manifesto, p. 115.

Torah. Something external is implied – legislation, tradition, an oral Torah. God could announce his will from heaven whenever uncertainty arises, but this is not his normal means of guidance either in the [Tanach] or in the [R.C.]. Nothing in the Bible suggests that God opposes accumulating knowledge and experience or creating guidelines and rules. It is only when these are misused that they become wrong. Yeshua did not object to 'tradition' as such when he criticized the P'rushim, but to 'your' tradition: 'By *your* tradition you make null and void the word of God!' – and he gave an example of what he meant.[291]

For traditional Judaism the scriptural basis for an authoritative system of Torah interpretation is Deuteronomy 17:12, which says that Israel is to consult and obey the priest or judge 'who is in office in those days.' This has made the ground for the entire system of rabbi-created law – which is understood not as being created anew but derived from what Moses received at Sinai and handed down to the elders.[292]

The R.C. adds another concept on the traditional idea of the Oral תּוֹרָה Torah based on Matthew 18:18-20. יֵשׁוּעַ Yeshua

291 Mark 7:8-13.

292 Stern, Messianic Jewish Manifesto, pp. 148-149. Also Dov Chaikin, gives a more detailed example of the slaughtering of animals. But I cannot agree with his reason for the introduction of the Oral Law by the Second Temple rabbinic establishment. But even if he were correct, to understand the Oral Law is indispensable for understanding much of the Written Torah as his own article clearly shows. Dov Chaikin, The Oral Law, Israel Today, March 2015, No.187, p. 24.

is speaking to those who have authority to regulate Messianic communal life (in the receding 3 verses). These people will have the right to establish *halakhah* (means the way to walk), as the terms 'bind' and 'permit' are used in first-century Judaism to 'prohibit' and 'permit.' These verses are saying in effect, "that when an issue is brought formally to a panel of two or three Messianic Community leaders, and they render a halakhic decision here on earth, they can be assured that the authority of God stands behind them."[293]

Tverberg contributes:

> How much can we know about the world of [Yeshua] anyhow? A wealth of literature actually exists that preserves Jewish thought from centuries before and after [the Messiah]. Best known are the Mishnah and the Talmud...of course Christians don't read these texts as authoritative, but they reveal an ancient river of thought that flowed through [Yeshua] world, which can fill in the gaps in our understanding. Other first-century documents like the writings of Josephus and the Dead Sea Scrolls shed light on [Yeshua's] world too.
>
> You might be surprised to learn that some of Judaism's most influential thinkers, including Hillel and Sammai (30 BC to AD 10), lived in the decades right around [Yeshua] time. Hillel's

293 Stern, Messianic Jewish Manifesto, pp. 149-151. This is a big subject which is beyond the scope of the paper, see pp. 149-154. See also Louis Goldberg, How Jewish is Christianity? pp. 140-148, David Stern, How Jewish is Christianity?, pp. 183-185.

grandson, Gamaliel, was Paul's teacher, who came to the defense of the early church in Acts 5:33-39. The words of these and other rabbis allow us to reconstruct the conversations going on around [Yeshua]. They use the same kind of logic to answer questions, interpret Scriptures, and weave parables, which yields fascinating clues to [Yeshua's] words.[294]

...Ken Bailey has spent decades travelling to the Middle East to study Arab peoples, showing how traditional societies there preserve the Bible's cultural perspective in ways that Western societies have not….

Christians may also be surprised at how Jewish traditions have preserved biblical attitudes...for much of the world, the culture of the Bible makes more sense than it does to us…

Throughout history people have lived in extended families, practised subsistence farming, and lived under the shadow of slavery and war. And around the world, many traditional cultures focus their children's training on sacred stories and order their lives around religious practices. With our individualism, secularism, materialism, and biblical illiteracy, we in the Western world are the ones who have moved farthest away from

294 Lois Tverberg, Walking in the Dust of Rabbi Jesus, p. 25. Hillel, Gamaliel, Paul and possibly even יֵשׁוּעַ Yeshua were Pharisees - so do not think of the Pharisees as 'the bad guys!' See Dr. Ron Moseley, Yeshua, pp. 95-96, 107, 140 and Brad Young's book, Paul the Jewish Theologian, 1997, USA.

> [Yeshua's] world. Could it be that we're the ones who have the most to learn?[295]

Jewish exegesis

Merril Bolender, continues, "God chose Israel to be His people. Because of this, He also chose their culture, their concepts and their language to communicate His massage." When the Greek and Hebrew mind both look at the same תּוֹרָה Torah they most often come to different conclusions because of different biases and use different methods of interpretation.[296] Brad Young begins by saying that

> the foundation of Scripture study and exposition, however, both in rabbinic literature and [R.C.], is rooted in Second Temple period and multi-faceted methods of interpretation developed by the Jewish people. One of the most important places to begin to understand the principles of interpretation is the system developed by Hillel the Elder (flourished ca. 20 B.C.E. to 12 C.E.). He enumerated seven distinct techniques for exposition that could be used to understand and apply the Torah in everyday life. These are rules for exegesis.

One difference in Jewish exegesis, Brad Young informs us, is its emphasis on text comparison (gezerah shavah).

> First and foremost, these rules of interpretation, or exegesis, focus on the Bible itself: the biblical text must be used to interpret the biblical text. Words in

---

295 Ibid., pp. 26-27.

296 Merril Bolender, pp. 20-21.

one text must be studied and compared to other texts where the same words appear. ...in order to interpret and apply the Bible to everyday life situations within the community of faith. The community, moreover is involved with the work of exposition and application. The preacher has one eye on the text, and the other eye on the congregation. Midrash breathes fresh meaning into the old text and makes it live for a new generation facing problems in a contemporary life setting. The great biblical scholar Martin Noth called the work of interpretation a 're-presentation' of the text. The interpreter is presenting again the old message for a new time.

In Judaism the process of 're-presentation' must be made legitimate by accepted methods and rules. ...Interpreting Scripture with Scripture according to the method of Hillel gained wide acceptance by those involved in the laboritous task of Bible commentary. Jewish midrash, or biblical exposition, explores the deeper meaning of the text. The method behind midrash is a sophisticated conceptual way of thinking about God and the sacred text inspired by Him.[297]

...The method of reasoning that claims this type of interconnectedness between verses in the biblical text is not acceptable within Western, systematic treatments of theological issues. Nevertheless, it is widely used in rabbinic literature and was certainly

---

297 Brad H. Young, Meet The Rabbis, pp. 165-166.

accepted by the early Jewish Christians in their approach to the sacred text.[298]

Young goes through the seven principles of Jewish interpretation[299] and his books show how these principles are worked out. יֵשׁוּעַ Yeshua Himself makes use of these (and frequently makes use of the oral תּוֹרָה Torah) so to know them helps understand יֵשׁוּעַ Yeshua words.[300] Going through Jewish exegesis is far beyond the scope of this book – that is why for anyone who seriously wants to study the R.C. it should be compulsory to read his two books 'Meet The Rabbis' and 'The Parables.' The reason being, he shows the stark contrasts between Christian hermeneutics verses Jewish hermeneutics. He shows the deficiency of the grammatical-historical exegesis (its necessary but not complete on its own) and shows the much deeper riches by knowing the oral תּוֹרָה Torah. Sometimes the oral תּוֹרָה Torah is intimately involved with the Parables.[301] That may be a big pill to swallow for some – that's why for an introduction to the subject it would be extremely helpful to read Young's books.

Studying the Bible without the help of Jewish sources is like building a house of wood and not painting it. Or having

---

298 Ibid., p. 168.

299 Brad H. Young, Meet The Rabbis, pp. 167-171; The Parables, pp. 28-29 list four disciplines of research that Young employs. For a more in-depth study see Rabbi Adin Even-Israel Steinsaltz, Reference Guide to the Talmud, pp. 211-222.

300 Rabbi Barney Kasdan, A Messianic Commentary on Matthew, p. 71. Moseley says that the Jewish writers of the R.C./Apostles 'clearly relied primarily in early rabbinic methods of interpretation' and cites John 1:1-18 as an example where John associates *Memra* (having 6 attributes) with the attributes of יֵשׁוּעַ, see Yeshua, pp. 133-134.

301 Young, The Parables, pp. 109-115.

a house with no pictures or furniture. Sure we will know enough to be saved but is that all we want? Have you ever heard of a professor never consulting other theology books? Can you imagine Michael L Brown, an expert in Jewish Christian apologetics, writer of over ten books, and a contributor to the Oxford Dictionary of Jewish Religion, not making good use of Rabbinic Literature? Young says how shocked he was to discover that R.C. studies for the most part ignore rabbinic literature.

> In fact, most Christians outside the academy do not know that such books exist! Even in the area of professional academic research, the evidence of rabbinic literature is marginalized...A biblical studies undergraduate major in most academic programs will not be introduced to rabbinic thought and literature, leaving a gaping hole in Christian education.
>
> ...Moreover, Christian scholarship is often characterized, sometimes unintentionally, by an anti-Jewish prejudice that sometimes emerges as blatant anti-Semitism...
>
> ...Christianity should not study rabbinics just to understand more clearly the [R.C.] environment. Rabbinic thought is relevant to every aspect of modern life. The literature explores the meaning of living life to its fullest, in right relationship with God and humanity. I believe that Christians particularly will enjoy studying the Talmud

> because ancient Judaism is the root that nourishes the branch...[302]

There is even a rabbinic parable dealing with the theme of stewardship[303] where the relationship between the Written and Oral תּוֹרָה Torah are debated. The parable shows however, that the purpose of Mishnah,

> is to refine the deeper meaning of the written Torah as it explores the mysteries of everyday living...employing Mishnah to understand the written word properly is good stewardship...[304]

In Jewish thought it is true that the Mishnah is often put on the same level as the Written תּוֹרָה Torah, yet, Young informs us, "it is not considered to possess the same authority as the Written Torah."[305] Stern also assures us that the Oral תּוֹרָה Torah is not equal to the Written as it must **submit** to the R.C.[306]

Rabbi Barney Kasdan settles matters well[307] saying that יֵשׁוּעַ Yeshua does not call Yisra'el to abandon the previous covenants nor their Biblical foundations. Instead יֵשׁוּעַ Yeshua challenges

`

302 Young, Meet The Rabbis, preface.

303 It's actually tied in with the parable of the Talents, Matt 25:14-30.

304 Young, The Parables, p. 90.

305 Brad Young as cited by Marvin Wilson, Exploring Our Hebraic Heritage, p. 49.

306 David H. Stern, Messianic Jewish Manifesto, p. 178.

307 Kasdan is referring to Matt 9:16-17; the old wine and old garments are pointing to the Mishnah and certain rabbinic interpretation of Torah.

Israel, and specifically the rabbis, to return to a more correct view of Torah and the Prophets without getting sidetracked by some traditions of men. I should say that most Jewish tradition is based upon the Scriptures, but this fact is easily forgotten.

For those of us within modern Messiah Judaism, it is important to note that we appreciate and express our faith in Yeshua, often through cultural expression of our Jewish heritage. We follow the model of the earliest followers of Yeshua, who walked according to the Torah and traditions of Judaism, the cultural expression of their faith (cf. Acts 21:20). It is also clear from the [R.C.] that the early Jewish believers (and Gentiles as well) followed much of rabbinic Jewish tradition.

On example of this is the fact that the third cup of the Passover *seder* meal is used by Yeshua to illustrate his redemptive work. This cup is not mentioned in the Torah details pertaining to Passover, but is actually a rabbinic idea added during Talmudic times. It would be surprising for some to realize that not only are the Jewish believers exhorted to remember the lessons of this cup (cf. Matthew 26:26-29), but the non-Jewish believers of Corinth are also (cf. 1 Corinthians 11:23-26).

So according to Yeshua's own words and the example of the first followers, we find a balance between the Bible and some extra-biblical cultural practices. With a proper biblical balance, many Messianic Jews would affirm the great blessing it is to don a *tallit* in prayer[308] with the knowledge of the Messiah's work for us! Similarly, what a joy it is to celebrate the feast days and many of the customs with the full picture of Messiah in view!

The fact that the Mashiach[309] has come clearly has implications for our perspective of *Torah* and tradition. Some of the classical rabbis anticipated this [in the Rabbinic literature]. This seems to me to provide balance in regard to a Jewish understanding of Yeshua. He came to elucidate the fullness of the teachings of the Torah, even to the point of correcting some of the errors in people's understanding of it.[310]

...it is clear that Yeshua took exception several times not to the written Torah but to some of the rabbinic interpretations of the Torah. Simply put, Yeshua never contradicted the Written Torah but was not afraid to oppose the Oral Torah (early Mishnah) when it was deemed necessary. In true prophetic fashion, Yeshua confronted any issue that distracted Israel from a purer form of Torah observance.[311]

Therefore we should not be afraid with, in Wilson's words,

---

308 Wearing a small prayer shawl that displays the **צִיצִת** tzitziyot, see page 127-128.

309 Messiah

310 Rabbi Barney Kasdan, Messianic Commentary on Matthew, 2011, USA, pp. 95-97.

311 Ibid., p. 121.

An exploration of commentaries, teachings, reflections, illustrations, and applications of the sages and early Rabbis that will be of interest and value for Christians intent on understanding the meaning of texts related to Hebrew heritage. The continual, dynamic shaping and reshaping of traditions rooted in the Bible of [Yeshua] is important for serious Christian study of the roots and early development of Christianity. This 'text within the text' will help illuminate, expand, enrich, and nuance some of the foundational – yet largely undiscovered – themes of Hebraic thought – especially those that emerged following the separation of church and synagogue. In addition, such study will provide needed insight for more effective interfaith dialogue on methodologies employed by Jewish teachers and on the similarities and differences between Judaism and Christianity. Finally, such study will lead to a greater appreciation of Yeshua the Jew and his *Aggadic* storytelling style so central to his parables and other teachings.

The Torah, both Written and the Oral, contrary to what some Christians have often taught, is viewed in Judaism as a means of blessing and living a productive and fulfilled life, as God intended it to be (Deut. 30:19, 20).[312]

Rabbinic literature assists us in understanding the **תּוֹרָה** Torah. "...most of the difficult passages or problems

312 Marvin Wilson, Exploring Our Hebraic Heritage, pp. 49-50.

confronted in the [R.C.] studies could be solved through a knowledge of Rabbinic Literature. Many of [Yeshua's] sayings have their parallels in Rabbinic Literature."[313] For example, Eli Lizorkin-Eyzenberg's commentary of John and Rabbi Barney Kasdan's commentary of Matthew both make very good use of the Mishnah as seen in footnotes and commentary. The insights they give are phenomenal. It is like instead of seeing a shed you see a castle. I'd say the same for Young and all those using Rabbinic literature. The input of Jewish scholars **on their own scriptures**, give "valuable and unique 'in-house' perspective from the very community who directly received, copied, preserved, and commented on those first scriptures."[314]

יֵשׁוּעַ Yeshua Himself observed the Oral תּוֹרָה Torah

"Unless you understand some simple things about the Talmud, you will never understand Yeshua's teachings." (Rabbbi Dr. Shmuel Safrai)[315]

Again, what may also be a shock to many is that **יֵשׁוּעַ** Yeshua Himself observed the Oral **תּוֹרָה**. First let us take a small snapshot of **יֵשׁוּעַ** Yeshua's life. The **בְּרִית חֲדָשָׁה** B'rit Chadashah (or as Alex Jacob would say, Apostles) shows **יֵשׁוּעַ** Yeshua as a typical Rabbi, travelling from place to place, depending upon the hospitality of others, teaching outdoors/indoors, in villages, in the synagogues

313 David Bivin and Roy Blizzard, Understanding the Difficult Words of Jesus, p. 43.

314 Marvin Wilson, Exploring Our Hebraic Heritage, p. 39.

315 Rabbbi Dr. Shmuel Safrai as cited by Rabbi Dr. D. Friedman: Rabbi Barney Kasdan, A Messianic Commentary on Matthew, Foreword.

and Temple, and disciples following Him – just like the many other Rabbis (perhaps 100's) of His day. יֵשׁוּעַ Yeshua style of teaching, methods of interpretation, and instruction were similar to other Rabbis. יֵשׁוּעַ Yeshua's parables, as mentioned before, were common among the rabbis. Rabbis also had disciples as did יֵשׁוּעַ Yeshua.[316] Based on the research of Jewish scholars David Flusser, Jules Isaac, Shmuel Safrai, and Pinchas Lapide; Christian scholars Robert Lindey, David Bivin, and Brad Young, and David Friedman,[317] it is clear that יֵשׁוּעַ Yeshua observed the Oral תּוֹרָה Torah. Bivin says that יֵשׁוּעַ Yeshua was never charged with breaking it neither but gave it great importance, citing Matthew 23:3 which included the Oral Torah and Matthew 5:18 which referred to the י yod or a קוֹץ tittle that יֵשׁוּעַ Yeshua would never take away. His speaking in this verse actually reflected similar rabbinic ideas. Even יֵשׁוּעַ Yeshua praying before meals is from the Oral תּוֹרָה Torah.[318]

It's interesting how Bivin brought this 'blessing' tradition up. Years ago at a conference I was told about how and why we pray the 'blessing' before and after a meal. Praying after a meal is based on Deuteronomy 8:10 so that's straight forward. But before a meal I was taught to *bless the food* which I did diligently most of my life. This was based on faulty readings of scripture. Jews though, bless **God.** To bless is way more then to thank; it is to adore, worship and

316 David Bivin, New Light on the Words of Jesus, pp. 9-14.

317 David Friedman, They Loved The Torah, p. 32. For an in-depth study of the subject, this is a very good book.

318 David Bivin, New Light on the Words of Jesus, pp. 44-46. See also Steve Maltz, Hebraic Church, p. 158 where he brings this 'blessing God' issue up.

praise. In the Psalms David blesses **יְהֹוָה** Yehovah[319] and Jews bless God for almost anything, good or bad.[320] So when we pray we need to be blessing **יְהֹוָה** Yehovah who provides the food – not the food. So when I pray I often pray the same prayer **יֵשׁוּעַ** would have said, **בָּרוּךְ אַתָּה יְהֹוָה אֱלֹהֵינוּ מֶלֶךְ הָעוֹלָם הַמּוֹצִא לֶחֶם מִן הָאָרֶץ** Blessed are you Lord our God king of the universe, who brings forth bread from the earth.[321] And the part we can conclude with is **בְּשֵׁם אֲדֹנֵנוּ יֵשׁוּעַ הַמָּשִׁיחַ** 'in the name of our Lord Yeshua Hamashiach.'

What **יֵשׁוּעַ** Yeshua wore would also indicate that he observed the Oral **תּוֹרָה** Torah. Like all observant Jews, **יֵשׁוּעַ** Yeshua wore **צִיצִת בִּגְדֵיהֶם** tzitzit (tzitziyot plural) on his garments, as commanded in Numbers 15:37-40 and Deuteronomy 22:12 and is illustrated in Matthew 9:20-21.[322] The woman who touched **יֵשׁוּעַ** Yeshua did not touch the 'hem' (KJV or fringe ESV or edge NIV) of his garment as erroneously stated by so many translations. (It is true that the English word *Hem* was a translation of the Greek word kraspedon meaning *a tassel of twisted wool* but modern dictionaries do not give this meaning so hem no longer can be used).[323] What were the translators thinking? Why did they not seek Jewish scholarship to investigate what could be going on here? Is this not what Young warned us about when he said, "Christian scholarship is often characterized,

---

319 See in particular Psalm 103, 104.

320 Lois Tverberg with Bruce Okkema, Listening to the Language of the Bible, p. 85-86.

321 John H. Dobson, Learn Biblical Hebrew, 2005, USA, p. 330.

322 David Bivin, New Light on the Words of Jesus, pp. 49-50; Eli Lizorkin-Eyzenberg, The Jewish Gospel of John, p. 47.

323 Dr. Ron Moseley, Yeshua, p. 21.

sometimes unintentionally, by an anti-Jewish prejudice that sometimes emerges as blatant anti-Semitism."? No, the woman touched the צִיצִת בִּגְדֵיהֶם tzitziyot (tassels or twisted cords; 'fringe' is getting close but the meaning is still too vague) on their garments. These tzitziyot are tied in a special way and have a unique appearance. Their purpose is to remind God's people to obey His commandments.[324] Like Stern or the Jewish R.C. editors, I don't think the word should be translated. Maltz and Lizorkin-Eyzenberg, also make a point that some words are not meant to be interpreted or translated. Their examples are חֶסֶד chesed and Ioudaioi,[325] (I would add the word שָׁלוֹם shalom[326]) and I totally agree with them. But the example above shows why it is time to start putting emphasis on Rabbinic scholarship! Actually, much of the meaning is lost with this story in Matthew if not using Rabbinic commentary.[327]

It's clear that יֵשׁוּעַ Yeshua had a thorough knowledge of the תּוֹרָה Torah both the Written and Oral and that at only

---

324 Stern, The Complete Jewish Study Bible, p. 1400; Steve Maltz, To Life! p. 156; Rabbi Adin Even-Israel Steinsaltz, Reference Guide to the Talmud, p. 444 (uses צִיצִית) and Phylacteries תְּפִילִין p. 445; Lois Tverberg with Bruce Okkema, Listening to the Language of the Bible, pp. 39-40.

325 Steve Maltz, Shalom, pp. 164, 168-169; Eli Lizorkin-Eyzenberg, The Jewish Gospel of John, pp. xii-xiii. **Chesed** means kind, loving kindness, kindness, mercy, favour etc. See also Strong's concordance entry 2617. **Ioudaioi** – translating as Jews 'sends the reader in the opposite direction from what the author intended.' Judeans is a better choice but still too vague. Yeshua was an Ioudaioi, a certain kind of Judean; from a group of Judeans.

326 The word **Shalom** has a much wider meaning than 'peace' as it means well-being, health, safety, prosperity, wholeness and completeness; Lois Tverberg with Bruce Okkema, Listening to the Language of the Bible, pp. 13-14.

327 For more in-depth meaning see Dr. Ron Moseley, Yeshua, pp. 20-22.

twelve years old He could astound the teachers with these תּוֹרָה Torahs. Jewish scholarship does have a huge advantage over the non-Jew. "What advantage has the Jew? ...Much in every way! In the first place, they were entrusted with the very words of God" (Romans 3:1-2). Romans 11:12 adds to this insight.

> If their stumbling is bringing riches to the world – that is, if Yisra'el's being placed temporarily in a condition less favored than that of Gentiles is bringing riches to the latter – how much more greater riches will Yisra'el in its fullness bring them!

Cranfield rightly informs us that this text is stressing the greatness of the benefits which result for the Gentiles first from the unbelief of the greater part of Israel and then, **much more**, from their ultimate conversion![328] Alex Jacob adds that,

> in addition to this, there was also a sense within Jewish understanding that the olive tree always produced its very best crop at the final harvest. So it seems probable there is within this a sense of the 'eschatological fulfilment' that Israel will be fully restored and will fully prosper within God's purposes at the final hour.[329]

The world has always benefited from the Jew, according to the Abrahamic Covenant, but now they are coming home and revival is beginning in Israel. Many are now accepting

328 C.E.B. Cranfield, Romans 9-16 commentary, p. 556.
329 Alex Jacob, The Case For Enlargement Theology, 2010, UK, p. 142.

יֵשׁוּעַ Yeshua and the more they do, praise God – will we ever be blessed!

The Renewed Covenant is totally Jewish

Bivin writes that the overwhelming majority of scholars subscribe to a Semitic origin for the gospels. He continues,

> Many Gospel expressions are not just poor Greek, but actually meaningless in Greek. One brief example will suffice to illustrate this fact. The text of Matthew 6:22-23 literally reads: 'The lamp of the body is the eye. If your eye is good, your whole body is full of light; but if your eye is bad your whole body is full of darkness...' The expression 'good eye' and 'bad eye' are common Hebrew idioms for 'generous' and 'miserly.' Greek has no such idioms, and in Greek this statement of [Yeshua] is meaningless, just as it is in English.[330]

The example above is called an idiom. Lamsa has compiled nearly 1000 idioms from the complete תּוֹרָה Torah.

> An idiom is a saying that foreigners cannot understand without being trained and is often taken literally and therefore misunderstood. This is because when we use an idiom we say one thing, but we mean another.

---

330 David Bivin and Roy Blizzard, Understanding the Difficult Words of Jesus, pp. 14-15. For more on the 'good eye' and 'bad eye' idiom, see Lois Tverberg, Walking in the Dust of Rabbi Jesus, pp. 69-76.

If you say "it's raining cats and dogs" to a Chinese person who is unfamiliar with anything English, he will not have a clue what you are talking about. In Aramaic if you say "If your hand offends you, cut it off." This means that if you are in the habit of stealing, cut it out/stop it.[331] In Matthew 20:22 יֵשׁוּעַ Yeshua asked, "Can you drink the cup that I am about to drink?" To drink a cup is an idiom for tasting or experiencing something.[332] Idioms are not to be taken literally but when reading Hebrew/Greek Scriptures how are most people going to even recognise an idiom. The Hebrew idioms in the R.C. were translated into Greek literally, that is why the translation does not give us the true meaning. If you have a poor grasp in the Hebrew language, culture and the oral Torah, then it will be extremely hard to recognise an idiom. You may only seem to know something doesn't make sense. This is a good reason to humble ourselves and let the 'Jewish' mind inform us. Blizzard remarked (as he was studying the R.C.) that

> It is difficult for us to understand or to grasp the implication of the word until we listen carefully to the teachings of [Yeshua] and to his contemporaries [that is the Mishnah etc].[333]

The idiom problem, has led to the realization that the Greek R.C. is partly to mostly a translation of Hebrew.[334] Garza informs us that the Greek R.C. is now believed by many scholars to be a translation from original Hebrew manuscripts.

---

331 Geoge M. Lamsa, Idioms in the Bible Explained and a key to the Original Gospels, 1985, USA, his introduction to the book.
332 Rabbi Barney Kasdan, A Messianic Commentary on Matthew, p. 224.
333 Blizzard, p. 24 (33).
334 Stern, Complete Jewish Study Bible, p. xl; Bivin, Gordon etc..

The inquiring Bible student soon realizes that the [R.C.] is undeniably Hebrew in grammar, idiom, and thinking. This opens up a whole new understanding of the essence of truth for the [R.C.] believer. If the [R.C.] is rooted in the Hebrew Language, then its teachings also derive from the Hebrew culture and are embedded in the Hebrew and not pagan Greek view of truth. The Hebrew language and thought are concrete while the Greek language and thought are abstract. This is why in the west there are so many different views of scripture. They are using the Greek language and thought to try to understand the Jewish scriptures. Rather then experiencing [Yehovah] in a real concrete manner they are searching for Him in a very abstract way. One needs only to consider that the writers were themselves Jewish, and while the language is Greek, the thoughts and idioms are also Jewish.

...The evidence will show that the [R.C.] was for the most part, written in Hebrew then translated into Aramaic and Greek. With this in conclusion we can then fully understand the [R.C.] Jewish scriptures and experience YHWH instead of searching for Him in the Greek culture. If one wishes to understand more precisely and with any real depth the language of Yeshua and His disciples, one should read His words either in the original language, as do the Jews with the Tanakh, or attempt to read it with 'middle-eastern glasses' or try to reasonably reconstruct it from the language at hand.[335]

Recent scholarship now concedes saying that the Hebrew syntax is embedded within the Greek text. The thought patterns behind the R.C. are Hebraic, not Aramaic or Greek and the scattered Aramaic words are either loan words or simply poorly transliterated Hebrew words and phrases rendered into Greek. The syntax or word relationships were as one would expect in Hebrew.[336] Then as mentioned before, the R.C. is full of idioms and puns which were very poorly dealt with by the Greek translators. Garza writes that of the over 5366 Greek manuscripts, each differing from the other and containing several hundred variants, in all these manuscripts are idioms/Hebraisms which are almost meaningless in any language, except in Hebrew. It had been argued that the problem was the poor Koine Greek, but actually the problem was not recognising the Greek as being a translation.[337] As these Hebraisms were often translated literally the most important tool to understand the Bible, therefore, is Hebrew; not Greek! In short, the entire R.C. can only be understood from a Hebraic perspective![338]

Nehemia Gordon has been able to compare the Greek Matthew with the Hebrew manuscripts, of which there are 28 manuscripts known to exist.[339] In Michael Rood's words he says that

---

335 Al Garza, pp. 6-7.

336 Al Garza, p. 21; David Bivin and Roy Blizzard, Understanding the Difficult Words of Jesus, foreword.

337 Al Garza, p. 36.

338 David Bivin and Roy Blizzard, Understanding the Difficult Words of Jesus, pp. 3-4.

339 Nehemia Gordon and Keith Johnson, A Prayer To Our Father, p. 41.

> he was astonished at the clarity of Yeshua's words in the original Hebrew language. The Greek text contained common 'Hebrew to Greek' translation errors that have caused the words of Yeshua to become critically distorted from what was accurately recorded in Hebrew.[340]

The many Hebraisms spoken by יֵשׁוּעַ Yeshua can only be understood when translated back into Hebrew.[341] Young agrees and calls this form of exegesis 'Linguistic examination'.

> The Semitisms of the Synoptic Gospels demand a careful study of the language of the text. Often the key to understanding the Greek of the Synoptics is to translate the text into (Mishnaic) Hebrew, using the best linguistic tools available for careful reconstruction of the language of the *Vorlage* (underlying text) of the Gospels.[342]

Often whole sentences and whole passages translate word for word into original Hebrew.[343] Hebrew scholars frequently notice how theses idioms enter our translations unnoticed because the translators do not even notice the Hebraisms. The problem is our seminaries that haven't

---

340 Nehemia Gordon as cited by Michael Rood, The Hebrew Yeshua vs. the Greek Jesus, p. xiv.

341 David Bivin and Roy Blizzard, Understanding the Difficult Words of Jesus, pp. 3-4.

342 Young, The Parables, p. 28. Eli Lizorkin-Eyzenberg does the same thing, The Jewish Gospel of John, p. 138.

343 David Bivin and Roy Blizzard, Understanding the Difficult Words of Jesus, p. 57.

understood that the entire R.C. can only be understood by knowing Hebrew well. It is now estimated that the percentage of the entire Bible originally written in Hebrew may have been over 90 percent. Again, it must be emphasized that the entire Bible has a culture, religion, traditions, and concepts that are entirely Hebrew![344]

> The assumption that the entire [R.C.] was originally communicated in Greek has led to a considerable amount of misunderstanding on the part of scholars and laypersons alike. Today, as a result of recent research, we know that the key to our understanding of this material is Hebrew. To this present day there has been a stress placed on the study of Greek and Hellenism. If any additional advances are to be made, especially in better understanding the words [of Yeshua], concentration must shift to the study of Hebrew history and culture, and above all, the Hebrew language.[345]

> It is most unfortunate that our Bible colleges and seminaries focus on Greek and Hellenistic theology, and fail, by and large, to equip their students with proper tools that would allow them to do serious biblical exegesis. A strong statement, to be sure; but sadly, all too true. It *cannot be overemphasized*, that the key to an understanding of the [R.C.] is a fluent knowledge of Hebrew and an intimate acquaintance with Jewish history, culture, and Rabbinic Literature.[346]

344 Ibid., pp. 4-5.

345 Ibid., p. 5.

346 David Bivin and Roy Blizzard, Understanding the Difficult Words of Jesus, pp. 15-16.

Gordon also discovered that Hebrew manuscripts had many Hebrew word puns.

> A *word pun* is a play on words that build on similar sounding Hebrew roots used multiple times with different meanings. They are a common feature of the Tanach and form an integral part of Hebrew story-telling. For example, the first man is named *Adam* אָדָם because he is taken out of the earth which in Hebrew is *Adamah* אֲדָמָה.

There is another word for earth but אֲדָמָה Adamah is used many times in Genesis 2 as a word pun. Word puns can be found on nearly every page of the Hebrew תּוֹרָה. Word puns are also found all over the Hebrew Matthew, proving that they are the R.C. originals, not the other way around as previously thought. The puns obviously cannot appear in the Greek.[347]

The early church also testify to a Semitic origin of at least some of the R.C., Papias, Ireneus, Origin, Eusebius, Pantaenus, and Jerome all testified to a Matthew Hebrew original from which the Greek version was translated. Isho'dad wrote that the book of Hebrews was first written in Hebrew and Clement of Alexandria said that it was translated by Luke into Greek. Eusebius added that some thought that, besides Luke, Clement himself translated the epistle. Jerome believed that Sha'ul wrote all his letters in Hebrew which were later translated into Greek. Epiphanius tells us that Jewish believers had Hebrew manuscripts of John and Acts. The Jerusalem and Babylonian Talmuds and

347 Nehemia Gordon, The Hebrew Yeshua vs. the Greek Jesus, p. 39.

the Tosefta also indicate the existence of R.C. Hebrew manuscripts.[348]

We Gentiles must make a dramatic shift – instead of relying on the commentaries of Greek thinking scholars, we need to shift to Jewish based scholarship. We also need to grasp the fact that "most difficult passages or problems confronted in [R.C.] studies could be solved through a knowledge of Rabbinic Literature. Many of [Yeshua's] sayings have their parallels in Rabbinic Literature."[349] Brad Young especially brings this out.[350] יֵשׁוּעַ Yeshua often spoke in parables[351] and Rabbinic Literature contains about 4000 parables[352] also, and they have many parallels to the parables of יֵשׁוּעַ Yeshua. These studies also confirm the fact that יֵשׁוּעַ Yeshua knew the Oral תּוֹרָה Torah very well.[353]

Not everyone agrees of course. Lizorkin-Eyzenberg believes the R.C. was written in Koine Judeo-Greek and cannot be described as just Koine Greek. That is, it is a Greek that has inherited the patterns of Semitic thought and expression – it retained many words, phrases, grammatical structures, and patterns of thought characteristic of the Hebrew Language. He disagrees that the [R.C.] was first written in Hebrew and then translated into Greek but instead he believes that the R.C. "was written in Greek by

348 Al Garza, The Hebrew New Testament, 2012, pp. 49-53.

349 David Bivin and Roy Blizzard, Understanding the Difficult Words of Jesus, p. 43.

350 Young, The Parables.

351 Perhaps 1/3 of all recorded words of Yeshua in the Synoptic Gospels are in parables. (Young, The Parables, p. 37.)

352 David Bivin, New Light on the Words of Jesus, p. 10.

353 David Bivin and Roy Blizzard, Understanding the Difficult Words of Jesus, pp. 47-52.

people who thought Jewishly and what is perhaps more important, multi-lingually." [354] I don't know how he reconciles this with the many claims that the church fathers clearly made that in their day there were copies of the original Hebrew manuscripts.[355] But it is not the purpose of this monograph to persuade the reader either way but as can be seen, a good knowledge of Hebrew is necessary to understand the "many words, phrases, grammatical structures, and patterns of thought characteristic of the Hebrew Language." As noted previously, the lack of Hebrew Jewish Scriptures is the fault of our ancestors such as the Crusaders and the Holocaust perpetrators who burned anything Jewish.[356]

After reading books penned by Young, Bivin, Stern, and Gordon it is obvious that one will conclude that the Gospels have mistranslations because of the underpinning Greek mindset. I want to point out to the reader that some of the mistranslations or lack of a Hebraic understanding can make a huge difference for your theological and world/life view. Some of these mistranslations are actually important. I will provide one example from Bivin and Blizzard. Let's go back to Matthew 5:17-18. Did **יֵשׁוּעַ** Yeshua come to destroy the law? Many Christians have thought so. **יֵשׁוּעַ** Yeshua's statement seems such a contradiction that many

354 Eli Lizorkin-Eyzenberg, Jewish Insights Into Scripture, pp. 30-31; Michael Brown, a born Jewish Scholar, also does not agree with Bivin. His paper is called, 'Recovering the 'Inspired Text'? An Assessment of the Work of the Jerusalem School in Light of Understanding the Difficult Words of Jesus.' I have not read the paper.

355 Nehemia Gordon and Keith Johnson, A Prayer To Our Father, pp. 28-29; David Bivin and Roy Blizzard, pp. 23-25; Al Garza, The Hebrew New Testament, pp. 49-53.

356 Wilson, Our Father Abraham, p. 99; Flannery, p. 104; Danby, The Mishnah, p. xxx.

commentators have come up with bizarre statements like "well the writer of Matthew did not really mean what he said" etc.. But His words are clear – as long as the world lasts, the **תּוֹרָה** Torah will last.[357] **יֵשׁוּעַ** Yeshua agreed with the rabbis that even as heaven and earth will pass away, not so the **תּוֹרָה** Torah.

> Other commentators have emphasised the word 'fulfil' in verse 17. According to their interpretation, something was lacking in the [Torah]. [Yeshua] completed or fulfilled the [Torah]. He did not do away with the [Torah]. He simply filled up what was lacking. And what was it that was lacking in the [Torah]? The Messiah. [Yeshua] fulfilled the [Torah], that is, he fulfilled the messianic prophesies found in the [Torah]. In other words, in [Yeshua], the [Torah] reached its zenith. Rather than being destroyed, it now existed as God originally intended. It had come to an end in one form, but continued in another, more perfect form.
>
> This interpretation has its problems. True, [Yeshua] is the fulfillment of the [Torah], but as previously noted, He had only fulfilled the messianic prophesies of the [Torah] that referred to His first coming] ...but is that the point that [Yeshua] is making in verse 17? If he is saying he is "the end of the [Torah]", then why does he say in the next verse

357 "Undoubtedly, this is one reason Judaism takes upon itself the responsibility to be the true Torah and to maintain it as part of the Jews' very existence. According to Judaism, God chose the Hebrews for the task of receiving and preserving the Torah, and this cannot be abrogated." Richard Bank, The Everything JUDAISM BOOK, p. 53.

> that the [Torah] would never disappear? If, in verse 17, [Yeshua] is stressing the messianic fulfillment of the [Torah], then verse 17 is in conflict with verse 18.
>
> There is something exasperating about trying to understand a verse like this. The meaning is apparently locked up. What the verse seems to say contradicts what we know from the other verses in the [R.C.]. The truth is that we cannot be expected to understand this verse. Like so many other verses in our English Gospels it is incomprehensible. Nor are we any better off with the Greek of this verse. The Greek is just as impenetrable. As usual, the only solution is to put the Greek back into Hebrew. Once we set this passage in its Hebrew context it makes sense.[358]

Everything hinges on the meaning 'destroy' and 'fulfil.' These two words are technical terms used in rabbinic argumentation. When one felt that a colleague had misinterpreted a passage of **תּוֹרָה** Torah, he would say, 'You are destroying the Torah!' And of course, his colleague would often disagree. Therefore what was 'destroying the Torah' for one was 'fulfilling' (ie correctly interpreting) the **תּוֹרָה** Torah for the other. In Matthew, we see a rabbinic discussion going on. Someone accused **יֵשׁוּעַ** Yeshua of 'destroying the Torah.' That did not mean that anyone was literally destroying the **תּוֹרָה** Torah, nor abolishing any of the Mosaic Torah. What is being questioned is **יֵשׁוּעַ** Yeshua's system of interpretation – His

358 David Bivin and Roy Blizzard, Understanding the Difficult Words of Jesus, pp. 111-113.

method of interpreting. So being accused, He responds strongly that His interpretation is actually more orthodox than His accuser. A 'light' commandment of not having hatred in your heart is as 'heavy' a commandment as not to murder. And one who breaks even a light commandment will be considered light (ie inferior) in יֵשׁוּעַ Yeshua's movement. יֵשׁוּעַ Yeshua is saying that no way would He abrogate the תּוֹרָה Torah by misinterpreting it. His intent is not to weaken or negate the תּוֹרָה Torah but to properly interpret יְהוָה Yehovah's Written Word; to then establish it making it more lasting. He would never invalidate the תּוֹרָה Torah by removing anything from it by bad interpretation. Even heaven and earth would disappear before something from the תּוֹרָה Torah was taken away. Not even a י yod or a קוֹץ tittle[359] will disappear from the תּוֹרָה Torah.[360] In Young's words יֵשׁוּעַ Yeshua is not rendering the תּוֹרָה Torah obsolete but is seeking to strengthen it through proper interpretation and application. "To fulfill" the תּוֹרָה Torah "means to interpret the message accurately and to live out the meaning of the text in practice."[361]

Then there are misuses of scripture. I noted previously that Jerome stated that the Jews take their name, not from Judah, but from the betrayer Judas. The church fathers and church leaders after them often misread the whole תּוֹרָה Torah to validate the persecution of the Jews. This shows how when our hearts are inclined to evil, how satan can deceive us.

---

359 The tittle of a yod is the small decorative spur projecting from the jot's upper edge. ל lamed can also have a tittle.

360 David Bivin and Roy Blizzard, Understanding the Difficult Words of Jesus, pp. 113-115; see also Brad H. Young, Meet The Rabbis, pp 42-45.

361 Brad H. Young, Meet The Rabbis, p. 43.

Bivin offers an extreme example with the misuse of John 15:6,

"If a man abide not in me, he is cast forth as a branch, and is withered; and men gather them, and cast them into the fire...(KJV)."

> For those who conducted the Spanish Inquisition, those not 'abiding in Christ' were the Conversos. If those false Christians were 'the branches fit for burning' of John 15:6, they undoubtedly were also the 'broken off' branches of Romans 11:17. Since God himself had broken off the branches mentioned in Romans 11, surely, the inquisitors must have thought, it was God's will that these deceivers confess their heresy and suffer their punishment. It made no difference to the lords of the Inquisition that branches in John's Gospel were actually runners or sprigs (Gr. Klemata) of a grapevine and not, as in Romans, branches (Gr. Kladoi) of an olive tree. The story of the perversion of John 15:6's interpretation should drive home to all Christians the importance of sound biblical scholarship and the enormous dangers inherent in wrongly interpreting Scripture.[362]

The name 'Christian' for the believing Jew

First of all, the name 'Christian' in the book of Acts was applied to Gentile believers by Gentile non-believers. Jewish believers called themselves **בַּדֶּרֶךְ הַהִיא** the Way (9:2; 19:9, 23; 22:4; 24:14, 22). Non-believing Jews called

362 David Bivin, New Light on the Words of Jesus, p. 153.

the Jewish believers נָצְרִים Notzrim (24:5) because they followed the נָצְרַת Nazaret (Nazarene, Matthew 2:23, 21:11). The word in modern Hebrew is also Notzrim.[363] Dr. Moseley suggests,

> The word *Christian* does not come from the Hebrew word for the *Anointed One* but from a Greek word, and it was not used by the Jerusalem Church at all. *Christian* was first used as a Gentile title for the believers at Antioch some forty to forty-five years into the first century (Acts 11:26). The term '*were called*' suggests that the name was coined by those outside the Church... There is no evidence that the term was used extensively as a self-designation by the early church, since it is only used three times in the [R.C.] and only once by a believer (Acts 11:26, 26:28 and 1 Peter 4:16).[364]

Arnold Fruchtenbaum adds that there was always a distinction in the R.C. between Jews and Gentiles who believed in Yeshua. Jewish believers were called Nazarenes, Gentiles believers were called Christians. [365] Kelvin Crombie contributes saying, that the movement of the followers of Yeshua were known as 'the Way', the Nazarenes', and later a stream was also known as 'the Ebionites' and Gentile believers became known as 'Christians. [366] Fruchtenbaum continues saying that the word Christian

---

363 Stern, Jewish New Testament Commentary, p. 262-263; Messianic Jewish Manifesto, p. 32.

364 Dr. Ron Moseley, Yeshua, pp. 12-13.

365 Arnold G. Fruchtenbaum, Hebrew Christianity, 1995, USA, p. 37.

366 Kelvin Crombie, In Covenant with Jesus, 2012, Australia, p. 301 #2.

> is no longer an ideal term to use for two reasons. First, not all who call themselves 'Christian' really are. The term is now used to describe a religious system rather than personal faith. Second, as said before, in Jewish history, most persecutions against the Jews were instigated and carried out by those who called themselves 'Christians.'[367]

Stern agrees saying that 'Christ' and 'Christian' are alien to Jewish culture and represent centuries of discrimination and persecution.[368] Fruchtenbaum might call a Jew who loves יֵשׁוּעַ Yeshua as a 'completed', 'true' or 'full' Jew.[369] Michael Brown also agrees and says that some prefer Messianic Jews (יְהוּדִים מָשִׁיחִים Yehudim Meshichim[370]) because it comes from Messiah which has meaning to the Jews; Christ and Christian are alien to Hebraic culture.[371] Alex Jacob adds that the name "Christian is heard by many, especially Rabbinic Jews, in terms of someone opposed to or separate from the Jews."[372] Jews who believe in יֵשׁוּעַ Yeshua call themselves Messianic Jews, Hebrew Christians, Jews for Jesus (but many people, Jew and Gentle, dislike that label), and there are other names. Gershon Nerel

---

367 Arnold G. Fruchtenbaum, Israelology: The Missing Link In Systematic Theology, p. 754; How Jewish is Christianity?, p. 127.

368 Stern, Jewish New Testament Commentary, p. 262; see also his Messianic Jewish Manifesto, pp. 14, 32, 82-84; Gershon Nerel, How Jewish is Christianity?, p. 96.

369 Fruchtenbaum, Israelology: The Missing Link In Systematic Theology, p. 707.

370 William Varner, How Jewish is Christianity?, p. 31; on the name of the movement *Messianic Judaism*, see pp. 29, 50 and Gershon Nerel, How Jewish is Christianity? p. 99.

371 Michael L Brown, Answering Jewish Objections to Jesus, Vol. One, pp. 11-12.

372 Alex Jacob, The Case For Enlargement Theology, p. 211.

believes the best word to adopt is תַּלְמִידִים talmidim (disciples) of יֵשׁוּעַ Yeshua or simply מַאֲמִינִים בְּיֵשׁוּעַ ma'aminim (believers) (in) be'Yeshua.[373] Believers in יֵשׁוּעַ Yeshua have different preferences. The most important thing to do though, is to ask individual Jews what they would prefer to be called when conversing with them.

The Name 'church' for the Believing Jew

In light of the negative connotations that the term 'church' has developed in the Jewish community because of what happened in Jewish history, it would be better to avoid this term altogether. There are other appropriate and acceptable terms, such as a congregation, assembly, etc."[374] Maltz contributes, "The actual word, 'Church' is a curious one, as the Greek word it comes from, *Kyriakon*, only appears twice[375] in the [R.C.], with the meaning, 'belonging to the Lord' (*the Lords*)." The Greek word, in these two verses, that becomes 'church' throughout these translations is *ekklesia*. But the word 'church' as we understand it, does not make sense in these translations! Ekklesia means 'called out' and the usual use at that time was an assembly. In Acts people met in private homes, a 'called out' assembly.[376] Ekklesia, temple or house of God in the R.C. never refers to a building. The church was Christ 'Himself in a different form;' it was 'an organic entity', a 'living

---

373 Gershon Nerel, How Jewish is Christianity?, p. 99.

374 Arnold G. Fruchtenbaum, Israelology: The Missing Link In Systematic Theology, p. 763; Eli Lizorkin-Eyzenberg, The Jewish Gospel of John, p. 154.

375 1 Corinthians 11:20 and Revelation 1:10.

376 Steve Maltz, To Life, pp. 14-15; Frank Viola and George Barna, Pagan Christianity, 2012, USA, p. 12. 'Called out' could refer to Egypt or sin, Stern, Jewish New Testament Commentary, p. 245.

breathing organism.'[377] The original church called themselves (הַהִיא) בַּדֶּרֶךְ The Way[378], a depiction of their function, a principle from the Hebrew scriptures. Church has been identified as a form (a physical building), rather than a function (the *called out ones* who meet (wherever they meet).[379] Church is not a *place* as *Christendom* has redefined it! It is a group of believers, so no we ought not send our misguided word 'church' to the Jews.

Blessing the Jewish people

Romans 15:25-27 says,

> But now I am going to Yerushalayim with aid for God's people there. For Macedonia and Achaia thought it would be good to make some contribution to the poor among God's people in Yerushalayim. They were pleased to do it, but the fact is that they owe it to them. For if the Gentiles have shared with the Jews in spiritual matters, the Gentiles clearly have a duty to help the Jews in material matters.

Such charity shows the close fellowship between Jewish Messianic followers and the Gentile believers. Gentile

---

377 Frank Viola and George Barna, Pagan Christianity, pp. xxii-xxiii. Viola and Barna believe that the church was not a clergy-led worship service attended by a passive laity, pp. 74-78 and Frank Viola, Insurgence, pp, 116-117.

378 Acts 9:2, 19:9, 22:4, 24:14, 22, 24:14. Stern, Jewish New Testament Commentary, p. 253.

379 Steve Maltz, Hebraic Church, pp. 56-57. The word church came from the Old English *cirice*, which took on the meaning of 'a religious building' due initially to the politics of Emperor Constantine – Shalom, pp. 84-87. I highly recommend this book.

believers are actually obligated to help the Jews in material matters, simply from the gratitude they should have for the gospel and the תוֹרָה Torah.[380] Cranfield comments that this collection was of great importance and would contribute to the cause of unity between the Gentiles and the Jews and as being an appropriate response to human need, an act of brotherly love. The Gentile churches are under obligation, debtors, to the Jews. For if the Christians have become partakers in the spiritual good things of the Jews, then they owe it to them as a debt that they should in return minister to them in practical matters.[381]

> Global support from non-Israelis, especially from Christians, helps the Jewish nation flourish and enjoy God's blessing leading to her being a blessing to the world. Humanitarian support for Israel is also needed, as the defence budget swallows up so much of the national budget. Christians support and friendship toward Israel is helping to change the negative impression Jewish people have about Christianity. There is no doubt that Israelis do see evangelicals as their friends, and this change in the historic relationship between Jews and Christians opens the doors to many discussions, not the least of which is the 'why' of the Gospel of [יֵשׁוּעַ] the Messiah.[382]

---

380 Stern, Jewish New Testament Commentary, p. 1629.

381 Cranfield, Romans 9-16, pp. 770, 773.

382 Mark L. Bailey, Israel the Church and the Middle East, p. 200. There is a concern that today's anti-Christian Zionists (those who oppose Christian Zionism; supersessionism is their underlying theological world-view) are damaging the image of Israel within the Church and causing people to have a poor attitude toward Israel. Mitch Glaser, pp. 101-111.

McCheyne[383] in a sermon reminded us that the whole **תּוֹרָה** Torah shows that God has a peculiar affection for Yisra'el and the simple question for you is, and for our church, "Should we not share with God in His peculiar affection for [Yisra'el]? If we are filled with the Spirit of God, should we not love as He loves? Should we not grave Israel upon the palms of our hands, and resolve that through our mercy they also may obtain mercy?" I pray that neither you or the church will turn against the Jew or the riches he has to offer.

Instead let us

נַחֲמוּ נַחֲמוּ עַמִּי יֹאמַר אֱלֹהֵיכֶם *"Comfort and keep comforting my people*, says your God."[384]

383 Robert Murray McCheyne (1813-1843) from a quote cited by Paul Richard Wilkinson, The Jews, Modern Israel and the New Supersessionism, pp. 101-102.

384 Isaiah 40:1.

Conclusion

Merril Bolender notes,

> For the past 19 centuries, the Church has totally failed to recognize that the Abrahamic covenant was an everlasting promise made by God Himself to the Jewish people. Instead, we selfishly and haughtily claimed all the promises made to the Jews solely as our own.
>
> Subsequently, rejection and persecution of the Jewish people were launched. This may be our chance to reconcile ourselves in these last days. God has given us the opportunity to show mercy, compassion and support for Israel before the final Day of Judgement arrives.
>
> In this present day, there is a worldwide atmosphere of antagonism, terrorism, and total misunderstanding of Israel. There are many within the Church linking themselves with those who condemn Israel, misinterpreting their true roots in the Jewish olive tree. Replacement Theology and Islamic theology are in harmony against Israel, both refusing to recognize that Israel exists. God's covenant with Israel is everlasting and unconditional. If it were not for this covenant, Israel would not exist today. God is a covenant keeping God and His promise to Israel will not be altered...
>
> Chuck Cohen states, 'Much of the Church has acted as though it has been grafted into a Christmas tree

– flashing its attractive lights and decoration, but unconcerned about its roots and wondering why it is spiritually drying up and dying. As God pushes Israel toward her final destiny, world hostility, ignorance and self-righteous hypocrisy will grow ever more strongly even in the church. It is not going to be easy to stand by the Word of God – but in the end it will be the only place worth standing.'[385]

...As Israel is being more and more isolated and rejected by the nations of the world, we, as a growing remnant have a window of opportunity to bless Israel, pray and intercede for her and be her friend during the difficult days ahead. I believe the harvest of the 'lost sheep of Israel' will come into the fold when the Church repents and takes her rightful role in welcoming her 'elder brothers' into the family of the redeemed through their Messiah [Yeshua].

...We live in a day of quick and unspeakable shakings. Our only way forward is to dwell fully in [Yeshua], to embrace the insight that the holy Hebraic scriptures reveal and to move in the fullness of His Spirit.

The Jewish people have a prophetic role in the unfolding redemptive purposes of God in the earth. The Church needs to explore, learn, understand and appreciate the hundreds of scriptures relating to

---

385 Merril Bolender, When The Cross Became A Sword, pp. 67-68.

> God's covenantal plans for [Yisra'el], His chosen people.
>
> As we study the scriptures, may our hearts be attuned to the heart of God's love for His people and how we, the Church, fit into His plan for [Yisra'el's] restoration.
>
> The Church is at a critical crossroads. The day of neutrality is the thing of the past…[386]

If we really do love the Lord, I think we are in a time to readjust some of our habits, attitudes and thinking. For a basic start we need to adopt a much more Hebraic mindset. This goes far beyond just using the name **יֵשׁוּעַ** Yeshua, cleaning up our vocabulary as mentioned above and knowing the Jews are a Holy people. From the concept of Hebrews 5:13-14 (milk and solid food), most of us at present will never get to the meat of the gospel without receiving the blessing of the Jews. To understand the R.C./Apostles we need to apply Jewish thinking and scholarship. At the moment many of us sometimes are only drinking sour milk as we are fed a Platonic, Aristotelian, Augustinian, and Hellenistic view of scripture. Frank Viola and George Barna call it a pagan Christianity.[387] There are plenty of books written on this very subject. We are in an age where we can do better. We have many available resources. But we need to put the **priority** on **Rabbinic** commentary. Greek thinking says we need to know *about* God; Hebrew thinking says we need to *know* God. Greek thinking puts emphasis on what we say; Hebraic thinking

---

386 Ibid., p. 69-70.
387 Frank Viola and George Barna, Pagan Christianity.

puts emphasis on what we do. If we are willing to allow the Judaic mindset to penetrate our mind, I believe we will be transformed in our minds to live not only holier lives but to present to the world and to the Jew a more appropriate and culturally relevant Gospel. Could we then be closer to making the Jews jealous, that they will receive their true Jewishness, which is in יֵשׁוּעַ Yeshua the Messiah? I wish all my readers a renewed journey and a true Hebraic Shalom!

For all those encouraged by this writing you may email me at leovanderploeg10@gmail.com

About the author

Leo Vanderploeg was born in Canada into a Bible believing family: he has two brothers and two sisters. Leo went to Dordt College, Iowa, USA where he took a major in Philosophy and minored in Church History. After serving as a self-employed bee-keeper for 10 years, he sold his business to do mission work in the North West Territories, India, Jamaica, Africa and finally in China, where he met his best friend Sue, from England. They are married with two grown up children and currently live in the UK. Leo is also the author of 'The War Opposing Creationism'.

L - #0095 - 070819 - C0 - 210/148/9 - PB - DID2584822